Usborne
POCK
NATURE

Silver

Contents

WILD ANIMALS

Barbara Cork

Designed by David Bennett, Anne Sharples,
Andrzej Bielecki and Nicky Wainwright
Cover design by Josephine Thompson

Illustrated by Denise Finney, David Wright,
Dee Morgan, Judy Friedlander and Ian Jackson

Edited by Laura Howell
Consultant editor: Miranda Stevenson
Language consultant: Gillian Ghate

Contents

Looking at wild mammals

When people say "animals", they usually mean mammals. This book is all about wild mammals. Mammals are different from all the other animals in the world. They are the only animals that have fur or hair. Female mammals are the only animals that make milk to feed their young. You are a mammal.

Fallow deer feeding her fawn

A mammal keeps the inside of its body at the same temperature, even when it is hot or cold outside.

Polar bears

A mammal has a good brain. This chimp is using a rock as a tool.

Chimp

All mammals breathe, even mammals that live in water.

Whale

All mammals have some fur or hair on their body.

Musk oxen have lots of hair. This keeps them warm.

Porcupines have special hard hairs, called quills.

Elephants have only a few hairs.

Many mammals' coats have two kinds of hair. Beavers have thick, short, soft hairs under a layer of long, rough hairs. Only the long hairs get wet in water.

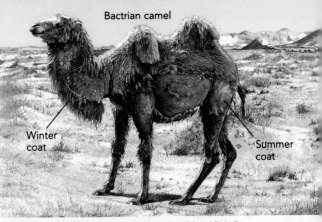

Bactrian camel

Some mammals, such as camels, grow two new coats every year. This camel is growing its thin summer coat. Its thick winter coat falls out so fast that the hair comes off in large chunks.

Winter coat

Summer coat

Go to www.usborne-quicklinks.com for a link to a Web site where you can find lots of useful and friendly information about mammals.

Legs and feet

Most mammals move around on four legs.

Ankle

Pandas walk on their whole foot.

Ankle

Foxes walk on their toes.

Ankle

Deers walk on their toe nails.

Back feet land in front of front feet.

A mountain hare's feet act like snowshoes. They are wide and flat and have lots of fur underneath. This helps the hare to walk or run over the snow without sinking in very far.

Otters use their tail to change direction.

Otters have skin between their toes. They can swim under water, using their feet like flippers.

Go to www.usborne-quicklinks.com for a link to a Web site where you can read descriptions of the different ways that mammals move on land, and in the water and air.

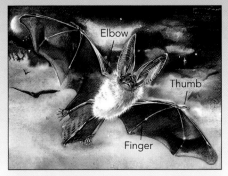

The only mammals that can fly are bats. They use their arms as wings. Thin skin is stretched over the long bones of the arm and fingers.

Kangaroo rats hop around on two legs. They use their long back feet to make huge leaps. Their tail helps them to balance.

Long, thin toes for holding onto branches

Spider monkeys use their strong tail like an extra arm or leg. They curl the tip of the tail around branches and use it to swing through the trees.

Teeth and feeding

Many mammals feed mainly on plants. They have a lot
of grinding teeth because plants are hard to chew.

Chipmunks
carry food
in cheek
pouches.

Hard pad is
under here.

The front teeth of a chipmunk never
stop growing. Its teeth do not get
too long, though, as it wears them
down when it feeds.

Bighorn sheep have no front teeth
in their top jaw. Instead, they have a
hard pad which they use to bite off
the tops of plants.

Giraffes use their
long tongue to
eat leaves from
tall trees.

Dik-diks eat
leaves from
bushes.

Zebras
graze
on grass.

Elands eat small plants.

Many different mammals can feed close together on the African grasslands.
This is because they eat different kinds of plants which grow at different
heights. You can see this if you look carefully at the mammals in the picture.

Go to **www.usborne-quicklinks.com** for a link to a Web site where you can meet some groups of
mammals in a forest who all eat different things.

Koalas feed only on the leaves of gum trees. They will die if they cannot find the right sort of gum tree to feed on.

Fruit

Dead vole

Long, sensitive fingers help to find and catch food.

Fish

Raccoons feed on plants and animals. They will eat living things or dead things. A raccoon can usually find enough to eat.

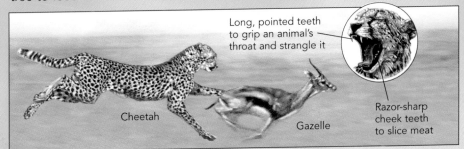

Long, pointed teeth to grip an animal's throat and strangle it

Cheetah

Gazelle

Razor-sharp cheek teeth to slice meat

Some mammals mainly eat other animals. They use lots of energy catching their food. Cheetahs may be too tired to eat for up to 15 minutes after they have killed. Meat is very nourishing, though, so they do not feed every day.

Mammals at night

More than half the mammals in the world come out at night.

Potto

Pupils open wide to let in lots of light.

Sticky pads on toes help to grip branches.

Many mammals have a special layer at the back of their eyes. This layer helps them to see in the dark. It makes their eyes glow if a light shines on them.

Badgers sniff the ground looking for earthworms and bugs to eat.

The tarsier has huge eyes and special ears that help it to see and hear well at night. It leaps through the trees, pouncing on bugs and small animals.

Badgers use their sharp sense of smell and good hearing to move around at night. They find food by sniffing the ground with their sensitive noses.

Go to **www.usborne-quicklinks.com** for a link to a Web site where you can find out more about bats, with pictures and activities.

Fold of skin

Many bats feed on insects that come out at night. This greater horseshoe bat eats flies and moths. It has sharp, pointed teeth to chop up its food.

Sugar gliders feed on flowers and insects at night. They stretch open folds of skin along the sides of their bodies to glide from tree to tree.

The red fox hunts at night. When it hears and smells a mouse in the grass, the fox leaps in the air like this. It will land with its front paws on the mouse.

Escaping from enemies

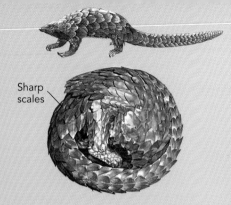

Squirrels escape from enemies by climbing trees. They are small and light and can leap onto very thin branches. Most of their enemies cannot follow.

Sharp scales

Pangolins have hard, overlapping scales all over their bodies. The back edge of each scale is sharp. When they roll into a tight ball, their enemies cannot hurt them.

1. This spiny anteater has sharp spines on its back. It burrows into the ground to escape from enemies.

2. It digs straight down with its long claws and sinks out of sight in about one minute.

3. When it is buried, its enemies leave it alone. The spines may cut them if they try to dig it up.

Go to www.usborne-quicklinks.com for a link to a Web site where you can play a game to identify how animals hide themselves.

Summer

Winter

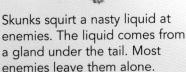

This skunk is holding its tail up to say "Go away, or I will squirt you with my smelly liquid."

Skunks squirt a nasty liquid at enemies. The liquid comes from a gland under the tail. Most enemies leave them alone.

A mountain hare lives in places where it snows in winter. It has a brown coat in summer and a white coat in winter. This helps it to hide from enemies.

Many mammals that live in forests or jungles have striped or spotted fur. They match the shades and patterns of the trees and bushes, so they are hard for enemies to spot. Can you find eight mammals hiding in this African jungle?

11

Homes

Mammals build homes to keep themselves warm, dry and safe from enemies.

Rabbits live in a maze of tunnels, which they dig under the ground. This is called a warren. They run into the warren to escape from enemies.

The female harvest mouse builds a home for her young. She tears grass leaves into strips and weaves them into a round nest. It is warm and dry.

The cubs are born in the middle of winter.

The female polar bear digs a cave of ice and snow, where she can spend the winter. She does not come out until the weather gets warmer in spring.

Go to **www.usborne-quicklinks.com** for a link to a Web site where you can explore the homes of many types of animals, including mammals.

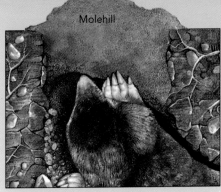
Molehill

The only home chimpanzees make is a nest where they can sleep. They bend branches over to make a bed of leaves near the top of a tree.

A mole spends most of its life inside its home. It uses its front feet like shovels to dig out tunnels in the soil. It feeds and sleeps in these tunnels.

Air hole

The home is called a lodge.

This is what a beaver's home looks like inside. The young are safe from enemies.

Underwater entrance

13

Finding a mate

Female mammals often give out a special smell when they are ready to mate. A male harvest mouse sniffs a female to see if she is ready to mate.

Siberian tigers

Tigers play together before they mate. This female is asking the male to mate with her. She bites him gently and then rubs her body against his.

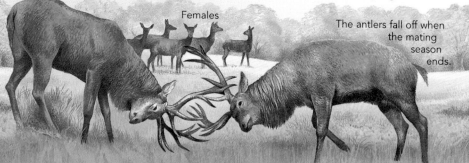

Females

The antlers fall off when the mating season ends.

Once a year, a male red deer rounds up a group of females for mating. He roars to tell other males how strong he is. If another male roars as often as he does, they fight with their antlers. The strongest male wins the females.

14

A male antelope, such as this Uganda kob, must dance in front of a female before she will mate with him.

Male   Female

1. The male kob holds his head up to show off the white patch under his chin. He stretches out his front legs to show off his black stripes.

Male   Female

2. Next, he holds his front leg out very stiff and straight. He taps the female gently with it. If she stands still, he will mate with her.

Male and female red foxes dance together before they mate. They stand on their back legs and hug each other with their front legs. They hold their mouths open and make a chattering call.

Go to www.usborne-quicklinks.com for a link to a Web site where you can see pictures showing how animals use signals to find a mate.

Having babies

After a female mammal has mated, a baby may start to grow inside her. Most baby mammals stay inside their mother until they have grown all the parts of their bodies. Then they are ready to be born.

Baby dormice are helpless when they are born. They are blind and deaf and have no hair on their bodies. They are born in a nest, warm and safe from enemies.

When zebras are born, they can see, hear and smell, and have hair all over their bodies. They can run about an hour after they are born. They stay close to other zebras. This helps to keep them safe from enemies.

Go to **www.usborne-quicklinks.com** for a link to a Web site where you can find friendly information and pictures of baby animals.

A few mammals are born before they grow all the parts of their bodies. Most of them finish developing in a pouch on their mother's body.

When a baby kangaroo is born, it is smaller than your little finger. It has to crawl up to its mother's pouch.

Close-up of the birth opening. The baby climbs upwards.

Looking inside the pouch

The baby holds onto a teat and sucks milk from its mother. It stays in the pouch for six months. By then, it has grown all the parts of its body.

The platypus and the spiny anteater are unusual mammals that lay eggs. A single baby grows inside each egg.

The nest is at the end of a long burrow in a river bank.

The platypus lays her eggs in a nest of leaves and grass. The eggs have a soft shell.

Growing up

Japanese macaque

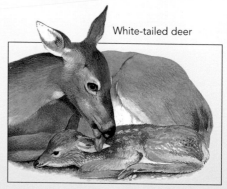

White-tailed deer

Most mammals spend a lot of time licking their young. This keeps them clean and healthy. It also forms a bond between mother and young.

A baby mammal sucks milk from glands on its mother's body. The glands produce milk as soon as a baby is born. The milk is rich in foods the baby needs.

A tigress picks up her cubs in her mouth to carry them to a safe place. The cubs do not get hurt as they keep still and their mother's jaws do not shut properly.

18

African elephant

Mountain goats play games with their mother and other young goats. This teaches them how to balance and climb on the steep mountain slopes.

This mother elephant is protecting her calf from an enemy. The young elephant is too small to look after itself. It stays close to its mother.

White-toothed shrews go out with their mother when they are about a week old. They hold on to each other in a long line so they do not get lost.

Go to www.usborne-quicklinks.com for a link to a Web site where you can watch videos of baby mammals in a real zoo.

19

Living in a group

Lions live in a group called a pride. The female lions are called lionesses. They do most of the hunting. They also feed the cubs and look after them. The male lions keep a safe area for the pride to live in.

An adult male has a thick mane. This protects his head and neck in fights. It also helps to attract a female.

Lionesses hunt in teams. They are more likely to catch large animals if they hunt together.

This is a young male. He will leave the pride when he is about three years old.

The cubs spend a lot of time playing. This helps them learn how to fight and hunt.

A lioness usually stays in the pride for life. She may feed any of the cubs. This helps them to survive.

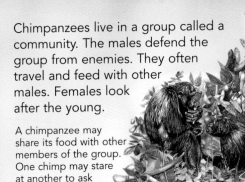

Chimpanzees live in a group called a community. The males defend the group from enemies. They often travel and feed with other males. Females look after the young.

A chimpanzee may share its food with other members of the group. One chimp may stare at another to ask for food.

There is a top male in each group. He often charges about like this making a lot of noise. This shows the other chimps he is in charge.

Chimps crouch down like this when they meet a more important chimp. This chimp may pat them to say "I will not attack you".

Woodland chimps catch termites by poking a grass stem into their nest. Young chimps learn how to do this by watching their parents.

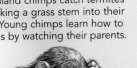

Chimpanzees spend a lot of time grooming their fur. This helps to keep them clean and healthy. Grooming also calms the chimps and helps them to stay good friends.

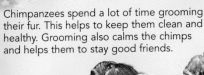

Go to www.usborne-quicklinks.com for a link to a Web site where you can find lots of fascinating facts about chimps, with a quiz to try.

Sea mammals

The only mammals that spend their whole lives in the sea are dolphins, whales and sea cows. They have few hairs and no back legs.

A dolphin's teeth are small and pointed. They are good for catching fish.

A dolphin comes to the surface to breathe air through its blowhole.

A dolphin's body is a good shape for moving fast in the water. It moves its strong tail up and down to push its body along. It uses its flippers and the fin on its back to change direction.

Mouth of a humpback whale

Bony plates

Manatees are a kind of sea cow.

Some whales have no teeth. Instead, they have rows of bony plates, which end in a thick, hairy fringe. The fringe strains tiny animals from the water.

This manatee calf is sucking milk from a teat near its mother's flipper. Manatees are born in the water and can swim as soon as they are born.

Seals, sea lions and walruses spend only part of their lives in the sea. They have back legs and most of them have a coat of short hair.

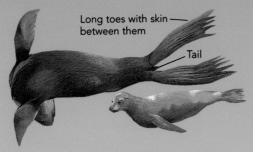

Long toes with skin between them

Tail

A sea lion's smooth, thin body helps it to swim fast under water. It uses its front flippers to push itself along. It uses its back flippers to change direction. It has only a short tail.

Walruses use their long teeth to dig up shellfish from the sea floor. They also use their teeth for fighting.

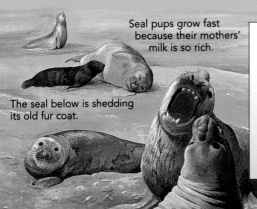

Seal pups grow fast because their mothers' milk is so rich.

The seal below is shedding its old fur coat.

Seals, sea lions and walruses leave the sea every year to mate, give birth and grow a new coat.

This is a group of elephant seals. The males fight each other to win an area of the beach. They will mate with all the females in their area.

Go to www.usborne-quicklinks.com for a link to a Web site where you can find facts and games about many kinds of sea mammals and other sea animals.

23

BIRDS

Rosamund Kidman Cox
Barbara Cork

Designed by David Bennett
and Nicky Wainwright
Cover design by Josephine Thompson

Illustrated by Roy Hutchison, Elaine Keenan,
Mick Loates, Andy Martin, Robert Morton,
Chris Shields, John Sibbick
and John Thompson-Steinkrauss

Edited by Laura Howell
Consultant editor: Peter Olney
Language consultant: Betty Root

Contents

Looking at birds

Most birds can fly. A bird in flight has a very smooth shape. This allows it to move quickly through the air.

A bird's wing has bones like an arm. It bends at the shoulder, elbow and wrist, just like yours.

This swallow's body is smooth and sleek. It can move very fast through the air.

A bird's wings are long and flat, like the wings of a plane.

A bird's wing bends in three places.

A bird needs a light body to be able to fly. Birds' bones are hollow, which makes them very light.

Inside a bird's bone

Birds have strong chest muscles to beat their wings. Some birds can flap thousands of times per minute.

Birds are the only animals in the world that have feathers.

Go to **www.usborne-quicklinks.com** for a link to a Web site where you can find fascinating facts about birds, with pictures too.

Birds have three kinds of feathers.

1. Down feathers
They help keep the bird warm.

2. Body feathers
They cover the body.

3. Flight feathers
They help the bird to fly.

Greylag goose

Down feathers are under the body feathers.

Body feathers

Flight feathers

Birds grow a new set of feathers every year.

A goose cannot fly while its new flight feathers are growing.

Baby goose

Down feathers

Baby birds have fluffy down feathers to help keep them warm.

29

Taking off and flying

Bee-eater

Humming-bird

Wood warbler

Blue tit

When birds want to take off, they leap into the air and flap their wings as fast as they can.

Mute swans

Some birds are too heavy to leap into the air. Before they can take off they have to run along flapping their wings.

Mallard

Tawny owl

Go to **www.usborne-quicklinks.com** for a link to a Web site where you can find information and pictures explaining what makes a bird such a good flyer.

Golden eagle

Eagles stretch out their
wide wings and float
on the air.

Large birds, like eagles, flap their wings slowly.
Small birds flap their wings very fast.

Kingfisher

Galah

A wing is like an arm. It
bends at the shoulder,
elbow and wrist.

Common tern

Birds twist or bend their wings to turn in the air. Look at
the way all the birds on this page are bending their wings.

Goldfinch

Albatross

29

Why do birds fly?

To build their nests in high places.

To go to warmer places, where there is more food.

To catch food in the air.

To look for food on the ground.

To escape from their enemies.

Go to www.usborne-quicklinks.com for a link to a Web site where you can look at amazing photographs of flying birds.

Why do birds land?

To feed or rest in trees.

To feed on the ground.

To drink.

To rest.

To feed their young.

To sit on eggs.

To meet other birds and mate.

Legs and feet

Puffin

Birds walk on their toes. They can run or hop along the ground.

Marabou stork

A bird's ankle is here.

A bird puts out its feet to land. It also spreads out its tail and wings to slow down.

Starling

This bird rests on branches. When it bends its legs, its toes lock onto the branch.

Some birds rest on the ground. Storks often sit like this when they rest.

Go to **www.usborne-quicklinks.com** for a link to a Web site where you can look at pictures of various birds' feet and find out what they do.

Birds often stand on one leg. They tuck the other leg under their feathers to keep it warm.

Coot

Mallard

Water birds have skin between their toes. The skin helps them to use their feet as paddles and to walk on mud without sinking in.

Snowy owls

The feathers on its feet help it to walk on the snow without sinking in.

The snowy owl has claws like daggers. It uses them to kill small animals. Its feet are covered with feathers to keep them warm.

Beaks and feeding

Birds have no teeth, so they cannot chew food. They swallow food whole and then grind it up in their stomachs.

Kookaburra

Black kite

This bird uses its hooked beak to tear up its food.

Shoveler

Strainer

This duck uses its beak as a strainer. It collects tiny plants and animals from the surface of the water.

Magpie

Pouch

Crossbill

A pelican uses its huge beak to scoop fish from the water. Its beak can hold more food than its stomach.

Rosella

Hummingbird

Go to **www.usborne-quicklinks.com** for a link to a Web site where you can see pictures of differently shaped birds' beaks and find out how they are used.

Birds have different kinds of beaks because they eat different things. The birds below eat different animals on the seashore.

Godwits poke their beaks a short way into the mud to catch small animals.

Curlews have very long beaks. They eat animals that live deep in the mud.

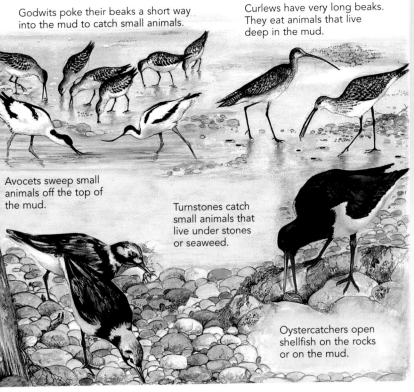

Woodpecker

Avocets sweep small animals off the top of the mud.

Turnstones catch small animals that live under stones or seaweed.

Splendid wren

Oystercatchers open shellfish on the rocks or on the mud.

Barn owl

Wigeon

Shapes and shades

Many birds match the leaves and branches of the trees they rest in. This helps them to hide from their enemies.

Birds are good at hiding. Can you see seven birds in this picture?

Frogmouth

When birds are sitting on eggs, they need to be hidden. This female nightjar is sitting on her eggs. She is hard to spot.

An Australian frogmouth sleeps all day in a tree. It sits very still with its head up. It looks just like a broken branch.

Birds may use patterns and markings to recognize each other.

Oystercatchers live together in big groups. If some of the birds fly off to a new feeding place, the others soon follow. They recognize each other by the way they look and the calls that they make.

Female

Males

Male and female mallards look different. Male mallards have bright feathers during the breeding season. They show them off in a special dance. This attracts a female for mating.

Go to **www.usborne-quicklinks.com** for a link to a Web site where you can find out how camouflage is used by many animals, including birds.

Song and dance

Birds sing most of all in the breeding season.

Male blackbirds sing to attract female blackbirds.

Female blackbird

A male blackbird also sings to tell other male blackbirds "This is where I live so keep away."

Tawny owls

Owls find each other in the dark by hooting.

Go to **www.usborne-quicklinks.com** for a link to a Web site where you can listen to many types of birdsong.

The male pigeon has to dance in front of the female before he can mate with her. He turns in circles and "coos" loudly all the time.

Female

Male

1. The male makes himself look big. He puffs out his neck feathers.

Female

Male

2. He spreads out his tail like a fan and bows to the female.

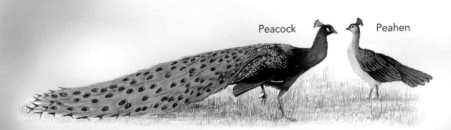

Peacock

Peahen

The peacock uses his long feathers in a dance to attract a female, called a peahen. The long feathers fall out when the breeding season is over.

39

Eggs and nests

Soon after a female bird has mated, she lays her eggs. If she kept all her eggs inside her until they were ready to hatch, she would probably be too heavy to fly.

Guillemot eggs

The female common tern lays her eggs on the ground. A baby tern grows inside each egg. The pattern on the eggs matches the ground around them. It is hard for enemies to see them.

Oystercatcher eggs

When baby terns hatch, they are covered with down. The down helps to keep them warm. If an enemy is nearby, the baby terns crouch down so they are difficult to see.

Rook eggs

Eider duck eggs

Go to www.usborne-quicklinks.com for a link to a Web site where you can see real baby birds being hatched inside nest boxes.

Most birds build nests. The nest hides the eggs and baby birds from enemies, and helps to keep them warm. Birds also sit on their eggs to keep them warm. If the eggs get cold, the baby birds inside will die.

Song thrushes

The male thrush feeds the female. She sits on the eggs for two weeks.

Baby birds that hatch in nests are naked and blind. Their parents look after them.

Rock warbler nest

Kingfisher nest

Golden oriole eggs

Hummingbird eggs

Growing up

Song thrush

Thrushes collect food from their home area near the nest.

Baby thrushes stay in the nest for two weeks until most of their feathers have grown.

Baby birds are always hungry. When their parents return with food, the babies open their beaks wide and call loudly. The parents drop food in their mouths.

Older herring gulls peck at the top of the beak.

Baby herring gulls peck the red spot to get a meal.

Herring gulls may have to fly far away to collect food for their babies. They swallow the food that they collect. When they get back, the babies peck their beaks to say "Feed me!" The parents cough up the food for the babies to eat.

Greylag goose with babies

Baby geese may watch their parents to find out what to eat.

They may sit on their mother's back if they are cold or tired.

A short time after they hatch, baby geese can swim. They will go into the water to escape from enemies.

Young geese grow all their feathers in about six weeks. Although they can fly, they have to learn how to move around in the air as well as take off and land.

Go to www.usborne-quicklinks.com for a link to a Web site where you can read the day-to-day story of a pair of owl parents raising chicks inside a nest box. You can also see pictures of the babies as they grow.

Resting and preening

At night most birds find a safe place to rest. They do not like flying at night because they cannot see well in the dark.

Hundreds of starlings often fly to the same place every evening. They all rest together for the night.

Some birds tuck their beaks under their wings when they sleep. They fluff out their feathers to keep themselves warm.

Sparrows

Lots of wrens may sleep together to keep warm.

When a bird bends its legs, its toes grip the branch, so it doesn't fall.

All birds keep their feathers clean and tidy. This is called preening. Most birds also spread oil on their feathers to keep them in good condition.

Herring gulls

Birds squeeze oil out of a gland just above the tail.

Oil gland

Lovebirds

Some birds preen each other.

Song thrush

Some birds have a bath.

Go to **www.usborne-quicklinks.com** for a link to a Web site where you can see many fascinating close-up pictures of feathers, and find out more about them.

Birds that do not fly

The ostrich is the largest bird in the world. It is too heavy to fly and it has only small wing feathers. The ostrich cannot fly away from enemies, but it can look after itself in other ways.

An ostrich is taller than a man. It can see enemies a long way away.

The beak of an ostrich is strong enough to crack the skull of an enemy.

The ostrich has long legs with strong muscles. It can run faster than its enemies.

On its big toe, it has a dangerous claw. It could kick an enemy to death.

Penguins do not fly with their wings. Instead, they use them to swim.

Rockhopper penguins

Penguins use their wings as flippers. They can swim very fast on top of the water or under the water.

These penguins are hunting for fish.

Penguins stick out their wings to help them balance.

Penguins use their wings and their beaks when they quarrel.

Penguins can jump out of the sea.

Go to www.usborne-quicklinks.com for a link to a Web site where you can find out about many kinds of penguins, with pictures.

47

FISH

Alwyne Wheeler

Designed by David Bennett, Anne Sharples,
Andrzej Bielecki and Candice Whatmore

Cover design by Josephine Thompson
Cover illustration by Isabel Bowring
Illustrated by Malcolm McGregor, Coral Sealey,
Martin Camm and Andrzej Bielecki

Edited by Sue Jacquemier,
Margaret Rostron and Laura Howell

Language consultant:
Gillian Ghate

Contents

What is a fish?

Fish are animals that live in water. They breathe through gills and have a skeleton inside the body. Their bodies usually stay at the same temperature as the water around them. Most fish lay eggs.

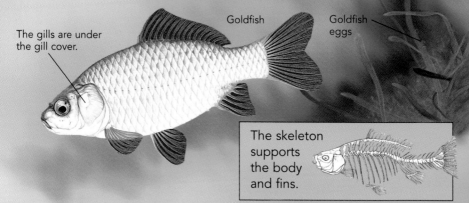

Goldfish

Goldfish eggs

The gills are under the gill cover.

The skeleton supports the body and fins.

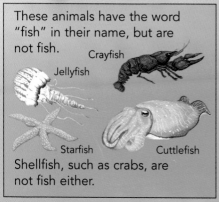

These animals have the word "fish" in their name, but are not fish.

Crayfish

Jellyfish

Starfish

Cuttlefish

Shellfish, such as crabs, are not fish either.

Whales and dolphins live in water, but they are not fish.

Humpback whale

They breathe with lungs. Female whales give birth to baby whales and produce milk to feed them.

There are three main kinds of fish.

1. Bony fish

Most fish have a skeleton made of bone. Their bodies are usually covered by very thin scales.

Bony fish have a gill cover.

Thin, overlapping scales (close-up)

Perch

2. Sharks and rays

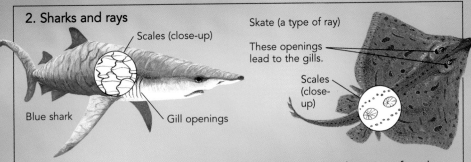

Scales (close-up)

Blue shark

Gill openings

Skate (a type of ray)

These openings lead to the gills.

Scales (close-up)

Sharks and rays have a skeleton made of cartilage. Cartilage is softer than bone, and can bend a little, but is still very tough. Sharks and rays are covered with lots of tiny scales. The scales are half buried in the skin.

3. Lampreys

Gill openings

Smooth skin with no scales

River lamprey – about 30cm (12in) long

Sucker disc (used for feeding)

Lampreys have no jaws and no scales. The skeleton is made of cartilage.

Go to **www.usborne-quicklinks.com** for a link to a Web site where you can find out lots about different types of fish, and print out some fish pictures.

How fish move

Most fish swim using their fins. Some fins move the body forwards. Others help to keep the fish the right way up.

The bass's tail sweeps from side to side. This pushes the fish forwards. The fins keep the body steady.

The manta ray has huge side fins. They beat up and down like wings. The fish "flies" through the water.

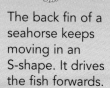

Back fin

The back fin of a seahorse keeps moving in an S-shape. It drives the fish forwards.

The eel's whole body wriggles to push the fish forwards.

Eels usually have small fins.

Go to **www.usborne-quicklinks.com** for a link to a Web site where you can find out more about the manta ray and other kinds of rays.

Some fish move in unusual ways.

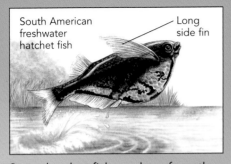

South American freshwater hatchet fish

Long side fin

Some hatchet fish can leap from the water. They beat their fins very fast to fly through the air. As they do this, the fins make a buzzing sound.

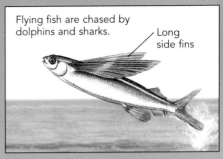

Flying fish are chased by dolphins and sharks.

Long side fins

Flying fish swim very fast under the water, using their tail fin. They burst through the surface and spread their fins to glide in the air.

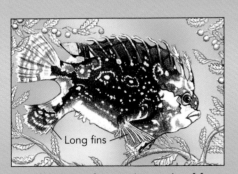

Long fins

Frogfish have fins at the ends of four short "arms". They crawl around among coral and seaweed looking for food.

Mud-skippers leave the water to catch insects on land.

They carry water in their gills for breathing.

Mud-skippers can jump. They curl their tail around against the mud, then jerk their body straight. The whole fish jumps forwards.

How fish breathe

Fish need a gas called oxygen to live. There is oxygen in water, and most fish get it by using their gills. The blood inside the gills takes in oxygen from the water.

Trout

Gill cover

The gills look like this when the gill cover is taken away. They are bright red because they contain a lot of blood.

The pictures below show how most fish breathe.

Mouth open

Mouth shut

Mouth shut

1. The fish gulps a big mouthful of water. Then it closes its mouth.

2. This pushes the water between the gills. The blood in the gills takes in the oxygen.

3. The blood carries oxygen around the body. The water comes out through the gill opening.

Go to **www.usborne-quicklinks.com** for a link to a Web site where you can read a friendly explanation of why fish can breathe under water but humans cannot.

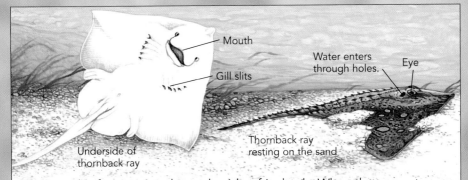

Mouth

Gill slits

Water enters through holes.

Eye

Underside of thornback ray

Thornback ray resting on the sand

The mouth of a ray is on the underside of its body. When the ray rests on the sand, it cannot gulp a mouthful of clean water. Instead, it takes in water through two holes on the top of its head. The water goes down over the gills and is pumped out through the gill slits.

Lungfish have lungs as well as gills. African lungfish usually live under water in lakes. They use their gills and lungs to breathe. They gulp air at the surface of the water.

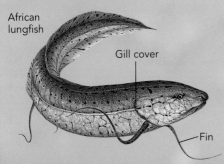

African lungfish

Gill cover

Fin

In hot weather, the lakes dry up. The lungfish buries itself in the mud. It uses its lungs to breathe air through a hole.

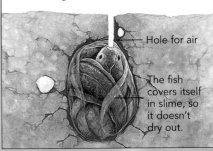

Hole for air

The fish covers itself in slime, so it doesn't dry out.

How fish find their way around

Like us, fish can smell, see, taste and hear. They also
have special senses to help them find their way around.

Smelling

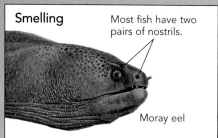

Most fish have two
pairs of nostrils.

Moray eel

A fish has a good sense of smell.
It uses its nostrils for smelling,
but not for breathing.

Seeing

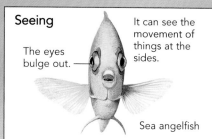

It can see the
movement of
things at the
sides.

The eyes
bulge out.

Sea angelfish

Fish can see very clearly in front
but not so well at the sides. Most
fish have good all-round vision.

Tasting and feeling

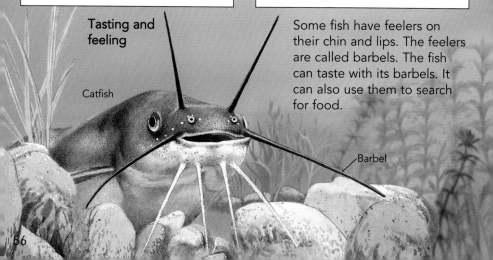

Catfish

Some fish have feelers on
their chin and lips. The feelers
are called barbels. The fish
can taste with its barbels. It
can also use them to search
for food.

Barbel

Hearing

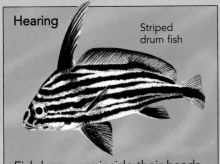

Striped drum fish

Fish have ears inside their heads. This drum fish lives in murky water, so hearing is more important to it than seeing. It finds other drum fish by making loud drumming noises.

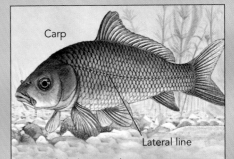

Carp

Lateral line

Most fish have a line running along each side of their body. It is called the lateral line. The little holes in the line can sense the movements made by other animals in the water.

A few fish have a special part of the body which makes electricity.

This elephant fish can electrify the water around it.

These lines show where the fish sends electricity.

As elephant fish move around, they notice anything which changes this electricity. This stops them from bumping into things. It also helps them to find each other. They can even sense things behind them.

Go to www.usborne-quicklinks.com for a link to a Web site where you can learn about many amazing animal senses, including those of fish.

Ways of catching food

Fish do not have regular meals. They eat what they can when they can. Some may go without food for days. Others catch food all the time. The shape of a fish's mouth often shows how it catches its food.

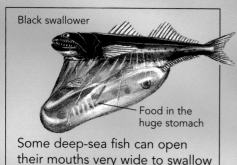

Black swallower

Food in the huge stomach

Some deep-sea fish can open their mouths very wide to swallow huge fish. Their stomachs stretch to hold their big meal.

Gill rakers

Basking shark

This shark swims with its mouth wide open. Its throat is lined with rows of curved cartilage called gill rakers. These catch tiny animals.

Great white shark

The great white shark is big and strong enough to catch almost anything in the sea. It has rows of sharp, triangular teeth. As each tooth wears away or falls out, a new tooth from the row behind it takes its place.

Some fish catch their food in cunning ways.

African freshwater
butterfly fish

This fish lies in wait just
under the surface of
the water. When an insect lands,
the fish leaps up to grab it.

Malaysian
archer fish

When the
insect falls into
the water, the
fish eats it.

This fish can spit water at
insects and spiders above the
surface. The tiny jet of water
knocks them off plants.

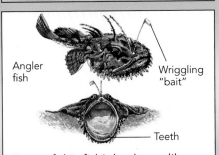

Angler
fish

Wriggling
"bait"

Teeth

Parts of this fish's body are like
a fishing rod and bait. Small
fish think the "bait" is food and
come near. The angler eats them.

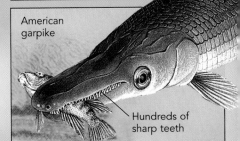

American
garpike

Hundreds of
sharp teeth

The garpike lies quietly at the
surface or in the weeds. When a
fish comes near, it turns slowly
to face its prey, then charges.

Go to www.usborne-quicklinks.com for a link to a Web site where you can find out more about sharks, nature's
most fearsome hunters.

Patterns

Many fish are covered with patterns of different kinds. In their natural surroundings, these markings help them to hide.

The mackerel's markings help it to avoid its enemies, such as birds and big fish. It is well camouflaged.

A mackerel has a dark blue pattern on its back.

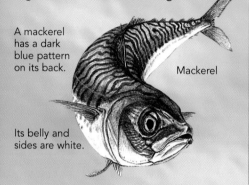

Mackerel

Its belly and sides are white.

If you look down on a mackerel from a boat, its blue back seems to merge with the water.

If you look up at a mackerel from below, its white belly seems to merge with the sky.

Some fish feed on other fish. This pike lies in wait among the reeds. The pattern on its body blends with the reeds, making it hard to see.

Many fish living on the sea bed can change the shade of their bodies. This Australian wobbegong (a shark) is blending with the sand and gravel.

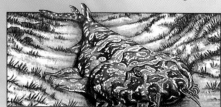

Some fish use their bright bodies or bold markings to trick their enemies or to warn them to keep away.

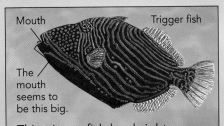

Mouth

Trigger fish

The mouth seems to be this big.

This trigger fish has bright orange markings on its lips and face. The mouth looks much bigger and fiercer than it really is. Other fish keep away.

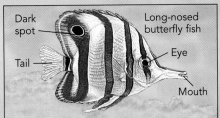

Dark spot

Long-nosed butterfly fish

Tail

Eye

Mouth

Many butterfly fish have a dark spot near their tail. It looks like an eye. This confuses other fish, because the head seems to be where the tail is.

This fish has spines on its back and a brightly striped body. The spines have poison in them and the patterns warn other fish to keep away.

Red lionfish

Go to www.usborne-quicklinks.com for a link to a Web site where you can find out about the many different ways that patterned bodies help fish to survive. Lots of good pictures.

61

Finding a mate and making a nest

Most fish just come together in groups to lay their eggs. In some types of fish, however, one male and one female form a pair. The male shows off to the female. This is called displaying.

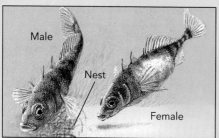

The male stickleback displays his red belly to the female. This coaxes her to lay eggs in the nest he has built. He drives other males away.

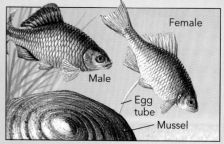

The male bitterling displays to the female and leads her to a live mussel. She lays her eggs inside it through a special egg-laying tube on her body.

The male dragonet is brilliantly patterned. He has a very big pointed fin on his back. He keeps lifting it to attract a female.

Go to **www.usborne-quicklinks.com** for a link to a Web site where you can find answers to dozens of questions about fish, including the subject of nests and eggs.

Some fish make a nest. Others just hide their eggs. But in both cases, the eggs are safe from being eaten or being washed away.

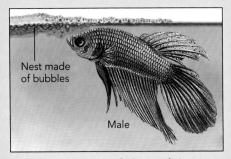

The male Siamese fighting fish makes a nest of bubbles at the water's surface. The female lays her eggs in the nest. The male guards it.

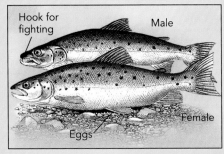

The female salmon scrapes a nest in the river gravel. The nest is called a redd. Males fight each other to win a female and her redd.

Californian grunion are brought onto the shore by the high tide after a new or full moon. They bury their eggs in the wet sand on the beach.

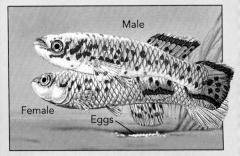

Lyretails live in small pools which often dry up. They bury their eggs in the mud. The baby fish do not hatch until it rains again.

Fish eggs and babies

Most fish lay lots of very small eggs. Some eggs float in the sea, and others stick to plants and rocks. The parents do not usually look after them.

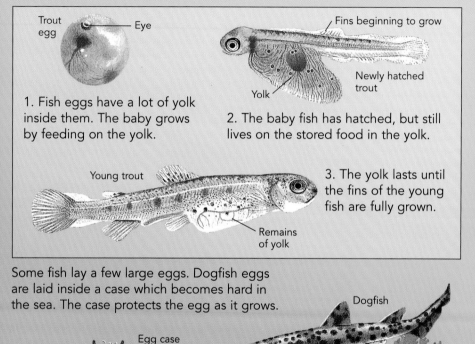

Trout egg — Eye

1. Fish eggs have a lot of yolk inside them. The baby grows by feeding on the yolk.

Fins beginning to grow

Newly hatched trout

Yolk

2. The baby fish has hatched, but still lives on the stored food in the yolk.

Young trout

3. The yolk lasts until the fins of the young fish are fully grown.

Remains of yolk

Some fish lay a few large eggs. Dogfish eggs are laid inside a case which becomes hard in the sea. The case protects the egg as it grows.

Dogfish

Egg case of dogfish

Some bony fish look after their eggs until the young hatch out.

Female

Baby guppy
being born

Male

The female guppy keeps her
eggs inside her body. The young
hatch just before they are born.

Male

Babies

Pouch

Male seahorses
carry the female's
eggs in a pouch
until they hatch.

Eggs

Male tilapias carry the eggs in
their mouth. They also shelter
the young fish in their mouth.

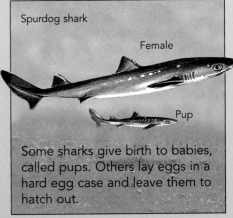

Spurdog shark

Female

Pup

Some sharks give birth to babies,
called pups. Others lay eggs in a
hard egg case and leave them to
hatch out.

Go to **www.usborne-quicklinks.com** for a link to a Web site where you can explore the amazing world of
seahorses, with pictures and facts.

Life in fresh water

Many different kinds of fish can live in the same river, because they like different parts of the river.

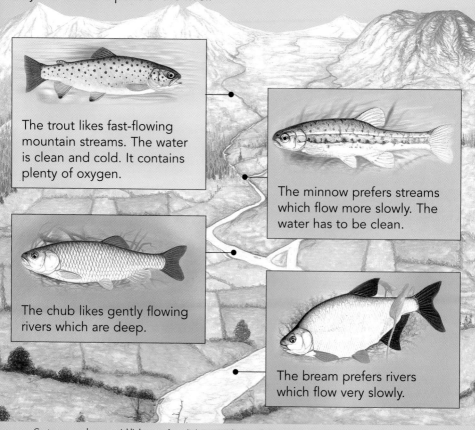

The trout likes fast-flowing mountain streams. The water is clean and cold. It contains plenty of oxygen.

The minnow prefers streams which flow more slowly. The water has to be clean.

The chub likes gently flowing rivers which are deep.

The bream prefers rivers which flow very slowly.

Go to **www.usborne-quicklinks.com** for a link to a Web site where you can take a look at three different freshwater environments and the fish that live in them.

Fighting the current

The water in some streams and rivers flows very fast. The fish must make sure that they are not swept away by the strong current.

Young salmon

Some fish hide behind stones to escape the current.

Asian hillstream loach

This fish is flat underneath. It can cling to big rocks on the stream bed.

Living in different environments

Some fish have unusual bodies which are suited to their environments.

South American freshwater angelfish

This fish is very thin. It lives in plant-filled rivers. It can swim between plant stems to hide from its enemies.

Blind tetra

This fish lives in freshwater lakes in caves. It has no eyes, but it can find its way around in the dark.

Life in the shallow seas

The shallow seas around the seashore have lots of food and hiding places for fish. Many different kinds of fish live there.

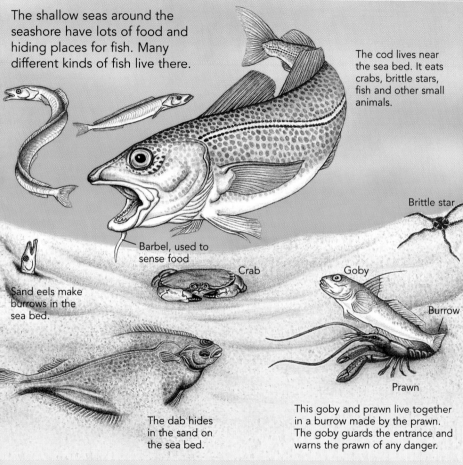

The cod lives near the sea bed. It eats crabs, brittle stars, fish and other small animals.

Brittle star

Barbel, used to sense food

Crab

Goby

Burrow

Sand eels make burrows in the sea bed.

Prawn

The dab hides in the sand on the sea bed.

This goby and prawn live together in a burrow made by the prawn. The goby guards the entrance and warns the prawn of any danger.

Go to **www.usborne-quicklinks.com** for a link to a Web site where you can explore a coral reef and meet the animals that live on it.

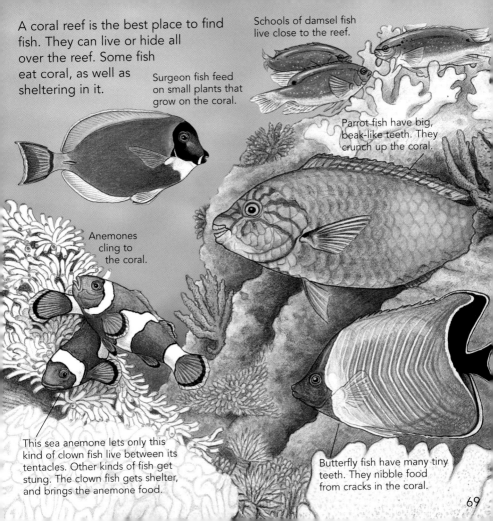

A coral reef is the best place to find fish. They can live or hide all over the reef. Some fish eat coral, as well as sheltering in it.

Surgeon fish feed on small plants that grow on the coral.

Schools of damsel fish live close to the reef.

Parrot fish have big, beak-like teeth. They crunch up the coral.

Anemones cling to the coral.

This sea anemone lets only this kind of clown fish live between its tentacles. Other kinds of fish get stung. The clown fish gets shelter, and brings the anemone food.

Butterfly fish have many tiny teeth. They nibble food from cracks in the coral.

69

Viper fish

Teeth

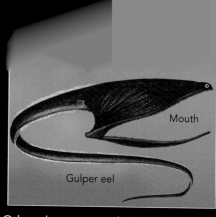

Mouth

Gulper eel

Some fish, like this viper fish, catch their prey with their big teeth.

Others have a mouth that is very big for the size of their body.

Many fish eat small animals which live on the ocean floor.

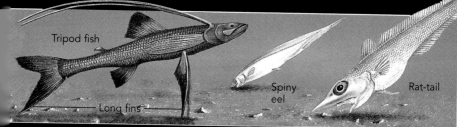

Tripod fish

Long fins

Spiny eel

Rat-tail

The tripod fish props itself up on its long fins. The bony rays in these fins can sense food buried in the mud.

These two fish swim with their heads down to find brittle stars and small animals that hide in the sea bed.

Go to www.usborne-quicklinks.com for a link to a Web site where you can meet some incredible deep-sea creatures.

Most deep-sea fish are black. Some of them have special parts of their bodies that make light. When these lights are turned off, the fish disappear into the darkness of the deep sea.

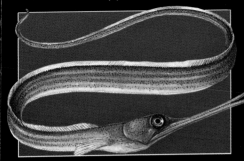

This snipe eel has no lights. It has large eyes, though, so it can see quite well in the dark. It feeds on tiny shrimp-like animals.

Deep-sea fish need ways of finding each other in the dark. Schools of lantern fish keep together by flashing their lights on and off.

The dragon fish has a red light and a green light near each eye. It uses these lights to find food.

This deep-sea angler fish has lights on waving stalks. It grabs other fish that are attracted to the lights.

CREEPY CRAWLIES

Cathy Kilpatrick

Designed by David Bennett, Anne Sharples,
Andrzej Bielecki and Leonard Le Rolland

Cover design by Josephine Thompson
Cover illustration by Isabel Bowring

Illustrated by Chris Shields, Denise Finney,
David Hurrell and Andrzej Bielecki

Edited by Sue Jacquemier and Laura Howell
Consultant editor: Michael Chinery
Language consultant: Gillian Ghate

Contents

Looking at creepy crawlies

This book is about animals called invertebrates, which means "no backbone". They have no skeleton inside their body. On these pages you can see the six groups of land invertebrates described in this book. Most of the different kinds of invertebrates are insects, but not all.

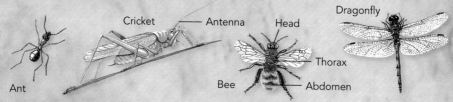

Cricket — Antenna   Head   Dragonfly

Ant   Bee   Thorax   Abdomen

These are just four of the different kinds of insects. All adult insects have six legs and three parts to their body. They have a head, a middle section called the thorax, and an end section called the abdomen. On the head are two feelers called antennae. Most insects have wings at some stage in their lives.

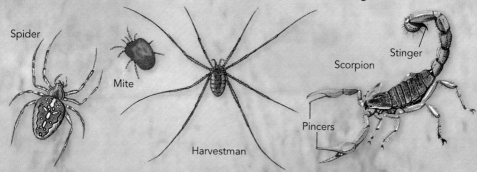

Spider   Mite   Harvestman   Scorpion   Stinger   Pincers

All these creatures are types of invertebrates called arachnids. Unlike insects, they have eight legs, and only one or two body parts. They never have wings.

Go to www.usborne-quicklinks.com for a link to a Web site where you can watch a short animated movie about insects.

Millipedes and centipedes are myriapods, meaning "many legs".

Millipede — Rounded body

Flat body

Feeler

Centipede

The body is divided into a head and many rings, called segments. Most centipedes have 30 legs, while some millipedes have up to 700. They both have feelers.

Woodlice and pill bugs belong to a group called crustaceans.

Woodlouse

Pill bug

Woodlice have flat bodies which are divided into segments. They have 14 legs for walking and two that are used for feeding. Pill bugs are woodlice that can curl into a ball.

Annelid worms, like the earthworms below, have bodies made of many segments.

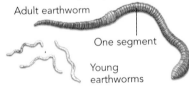

Adult earthworm

One segment

Young earthworms

Earthworms have no feelers and never have legs. They have no obvious head, but they do have a mouth opening at the front end.

Slugs and snails are types of invertebrates called gastropods.

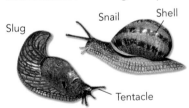

Snail — Shell

Slug

Tentacle

They both move on a muscular "foot" and have one or two pairs of tentacles. Snails have a shell on their back but slugs do not.

How invertebrates move

Many insects can fly, using one or two pairs of wings. Some can fly very fast – a dragonfly can reach 40km (25 miles) an hour.

A beetle has two pairs of wings.

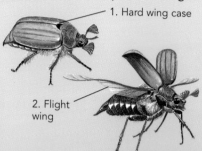

1. Hard wing case

2. Flight wing

Beetles use one pair of wings when they fly. They hold their wing cases out of the way and move the flight wings up and down.

Bees use two pairs of wings in flight but it looks like one pair. Tiny hooks join the pairs of wings together.

Hook

Flight wing

Balancer

Flies have a second pair of tiny wings to help them balance.

How the wings move in flight

During the down stroke, the wings push the air down and back, moving the insect through the air.

1. 2. 3. 4.

Go to **www.usborne-quicklinks.com** for a link to a Web site where you can learn more about a worm's body with Squirmin' Herman the worm.

This looper caterpillar brings its back legs to the front, then moves the front legs forwards.

It has no legs along the middle of its body.

Front legs

Back legs

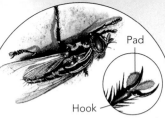

Pad

Hook

A fly has suction pads and hooks on its feet. It can use them to walk upside down.

Grasshopper

A grasshopper can jump 20 times its body length. It can use its wings to glide further.

Long, strong back legs

Most caterpillars have several pairs of legs. They move each pair a little in turn.

The front end is moving forwards.

Tiny bristles on the worm's body help it to grip the soil.

An earthworm crawls along by using its muscles. It moves by making parts of its body longer and thinner and then shorter and fatter.

How invertebrates feed

There are thousands of different invertebrates. They do not all find food or eat in the same way. Some eat plants, some eat animals and others eat both. A few invertebrates feed on blood.

Butterflies and moths feed on sweet nectar from inside flowers.

Feeding tube

They suck the nectar through a feeding tube.

The tube is curled up when the insect is not feeding.

Pliers

A grasshopper's jaws work like pliers to nip off bits of grass.

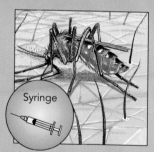

Syringe

A female mosquito pierces skin and sucks up blood, like a syringe.

Sponge

The mouthparts of a fly soak up liquids like a sponge mops up water.

Go to www.usborne-quicklinks.com for a link to a Web site where you can look at amazing pictures of insects' heads and mouths through a powerful microscope.

This hairy tarantula is a giant spider. It lives in hot places in America. It feeds on small mammals, insects and small snakes.

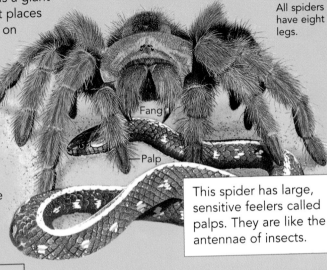

Tarantula

All spiders have eight legs.

Fang

Palp

Snake

Poison from the spider's fangs prevents its victim from moving. Then the spider sucks the victim's insides dry.

This spider has large, sensitive feelers called palps. They are like the antennae of insects.

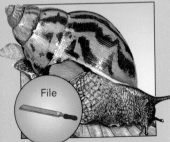

File

A snail's tongue is like a rough file. It feeds on leaves, fruit and flowers.

Burying beetles feed on dead animals. Females also lay their eggs on the body once it is buried. The young feed on the body when they hatch.

Burying beetles

These beetles dig soil from under a dead bird, so it is slowly buried.

79

Staying safe

Many invertebrates are difficult to see, because they match their surroundings. Some have bright bodies which warn enemies not to touch. Others squirt harmful chemicals.

The thorn bug looks like a thorn on a twig.

This looper caterpillar looks like a twig.

The peppered moth is almost invisible on this tree trunk.

A leaf butterfly looks like a leaf when it is resting.

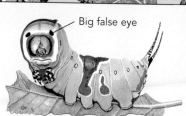

Big false eye

The puss moth caterpillar is camouflaged by its green body. It can also scare birds away by rearing its bright face and its tail.

Abdomen

Front leg

The flower mantis looks like the flower on which it sits. Insects come to the flower to feed and get trapped by the mantis.

Go to **www.usborne-quicklinks.com** for a link to a Web site where you can look at photographs and cartoons to learn how butterflies and moths defend themselves.

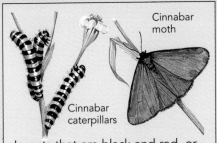

Cinnabar moth

Cinnabar caterpillars

Insects that are black and red, or yellow and black, usually taste bad. Birds learn to avoid them.

Acid

This wood ant is ready for battle. In this position it can squirt acid at enemies that come too near.

If it is startled, the bombardier beetle fires a gas from its rear that irritates the eyes of an enemy. The gas pops and also forms a smoke screen. The beetle escapes while the enemy is confused. This drives off most enemies, from ants, spiders and beetles to frogs and toads.

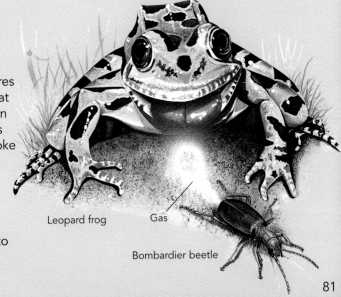

Leopard frog

Gas

Bombardier beetle

81

Eggs and young

Most female invertebrates lay eggs. These are usually quite small. The eggs are laid alone or in groups, in different places. Usually each egg is put where there is food for the young when it hatches.

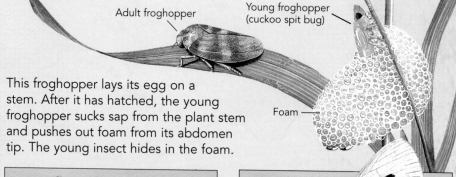

Adult froghopper

Young froghopper (cuckoo spit bug)

Foam

This froghopper lays its egg on a stem. After it has hatched, the young froghopper sucks sap from the plant stem and pushes out foam from its abdomen tip. The young insect hides in the foam.

Wolf spider

Eggs in silk cocoon

This female wolf spider spins a silk cocoon for her eggs. She carries it in her jaws until the eggs hatch.

Cabbage white butterfly

Eggs

Cabbage leaf

A female butterfly lays her eggs on a leaf. The caterpillars hatch and feed on it. The mother does not look after her eggs or young.

Go to www.usborne-quicklinks.com for a link to a Web site where you can find out how some types of wasps lay their eggs on caterpillars.

Caterpillar

Potter wasp

The wasp makes this pot of clay.

The potter wasp catches and poisons caterpillars. Then she pushes them into her clay pot. When it is full, she lays an egg inside. When the wasp grub hatches, it feeds on the caterpillars.

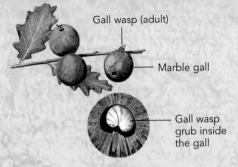

Gall wasp (adult)

Marble gall

Gall wasp grub inside the gall

A marble gall is made by a wasp that lays its egg in the bud of an oak. The bud swells around the grub and forms a lump called a gall. The wasp grub feeds on the gall until it changes into an adult wasp.

Garden snail

Eggs

A snail lays a lot of eggs in the soil, then leaves them to hatch by themselves. The young look like very tiny snails.

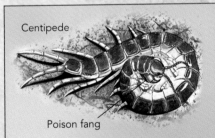

Centipede

Poison fang

Some female centipedes coil around their eggs in the soil and protect them fiercely. They will stab intruders with their fangs.

83

Growing up

Young invertebrates often look different from their parents. They change their appearance at least once before becoming adults. Other young invertebrates look like their parents when they are born or hatched.

Adult aphid

Baby

Eggs

Young snail

Some aphids do not lay eggs at all. They can give birth to live babies without mating. The babies are tiny versions of their mother.

Female snails lay eggs. When the young hatch out, they look like very tiny adults. Their shells grow as the snails get bigger.

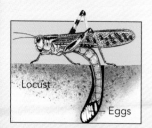

Locust

Eggs

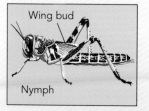

Wing bud

Nymph

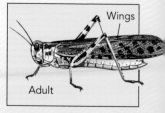

Wings

Adult

1. A female locust lays her eggs in damp, warm soil and leaves them to hatch.

2. The young locust (nymph) looks like an adult but has no wings, only wing buds.

3. The nymph grows and changes into an adult. The adult has wings and can fly.

Go to **www.usborne-quicklinks.com** for a link to a Web site where you can watch a video about the mayfly, an insect which lives for a year as a nymph but less than a day as an adult.

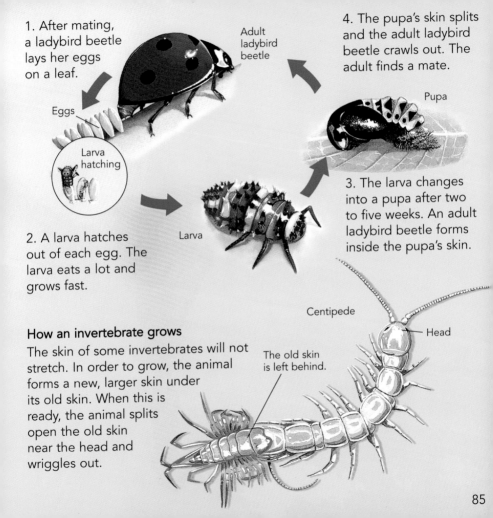

1. After mating, a ladybird beetle lays her eggs on a leaf.

Eggs

Adult ladybird beetle

Larva hatching

2. A larva hatches out of each egg. The larva eats a lot and grows fast.

Larva

4. The pupa's skin splits and the adult ladybird beetle crawls out. The adult finds a mate.

Pupa

3. The larva changes into a pupa after two to five weeks. An adult ladybird beetle forms inside the pupa's skin.

How an invertebrate grows

The skin of some invertebrates will not stretch. In order to grow, the animal forms a new, larger skin under its old skin. When this is ready, the animal splits open the old skin near the head and wriggles out.

Centipede

Head

The old skin is left behind.

Spiders

Spiders live in many different places, from mountains or deserts to people's houses. Most of the 60,000 different kinds of spiders are very useful. They eat lots of flies and other pests. All spiders have eight legs and spin silk.

Silk is made by special organs in the abdomen.

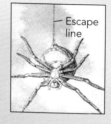

Escape line

This spider spins a silk thread as an escape line.

This spider wraps its prey in silken threads.

Cocoon

Spiders protect their eggs with a silk cocoon.

An orb spider waits for its prey to become trapped in its web. The spider does not get stuck on its own web because it has oil on its feet.

Web

The crab spider below looks like the flower it sits on. It lies in wait for passing insects such as bees, then grabs one in its fangs.

Deadly spiders

All spiders have fangs with poison to stun or kill their prey. A few spiders are dangerous and can hurt people. Here are three of them.

The red back of Australia is called the night stinger in New Zealand. Females have a poisonous bite.

The female black widow is one of the most feared spiders in the United States. Her bite can kill.

This funnel web spider lives around Sydney in Australia.

The web-throwing spider spins a net of sticky silk threads. It waits for its prey to walk under it. Then it throws the net over the prey.

Net

The trapdoor spider waits in its trap until the prey is close. Then it strikes and drags the insect down into its silk-lined tunnel. The trapdoor shuts tight and the prey is killed.

Trapdoor

Trapdoor spider

Grasshopper (prey)

Go to **www.usborne-quicklinks.com** for a link to a Web site where you can find out about many different kinds of spiders, then try a word search or a quiz.

Slugs and snails

Slugs and snails belong to a group of animals called gastropods. This means "bellyfoots". Slugs are land snails that have no shell.

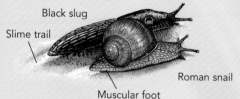

Black slug

Slime trail

Roman snail

Muscular foot

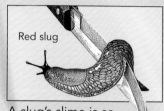

Red slug

Slugs and snails make a slimy substance that helps them move along. They leave a slime trail. The flat underpart of their body is called a muscular foot.

A slug's slime is so protective that it can climb over a very sharp knife unharmed.

Great grey slug

Pointed snail

Slugs and snails live in damp places among plants, under stones, or in the soil.

Banded snail

Garden snails

Plug

When the weather is very dry or cold, the snail pulls its body inside its shell. Its slime hardens and forms a plug so that the snail is sealed inside. When the weather improves, the plug softens.

Go to **www.usborne-quicklinks.com** for a link to a Web site where you can find lots of facts about snails, with activities and pictures.

There are giant snails in many parts of the world. This one comes from West Africa. One of the largest snails ever found measured 34cm (13in) from the top of its shell to the tip of its head. Giant snails eat all kinds of plants and their fruits, including bananas.

The long tentacles have eyes at their tips. They do not see things as we do. A snail can tell only light from dark.

Tentacle

Eye

Young African giant snail

A young snail looks just like its parent.

Tentacle

The short tentacles smell and feel things. They have no eyes.

Beetles

There are over 250,000 different kinds of beetles. If you turn over a log in a forest or disturb some fallen leaves, you are likely to find a beetle.

Most beetles are quite small. But a few grow much bigger, like the beetles on the right.

These beetles are shown at just under half their real size.

Actual size

Flea beetle

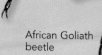

African Goliath beetle

American Hercules beetle

The flea beetle above is one of the smallest beetles in the world.

The heaviest beetle in the world is one like this. It weighs 100g (3½oz).

The longest beetle in the world is one like this. It is 19cm (7½in) long.

Go to **www.usborne-quicklinks.com** for a link to a Web site where you can put together a beetle puzzle, then learn some facts about different types of beetles.

Helpful beetles

The beetle below was brought into America from its home in Australia. It eats the scale insect pests that damage orange and lemon trees in California.

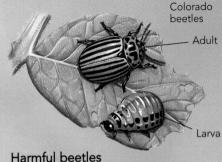

Colorado beetles

Adult

Larva

Scale insect

Australian cardinal beetle

Orange

Harmful beetles

Colorado beetles and their larvae eat the leaves of potato plants. Their home is in the United States but they have been found in most places where potatoes are grown. They can destroy a whole potato crop.

Living lanterns

Fireflies and glow-worms are not flies or worms. They are beetles. Both insects can produce light at the tip of their bodies. They use light to attract a mate. In hot countries you can see trees lit up by fireflies flashing.

Firefly

Glow-worm

Termite cities

Some insects live and work together in large family groups. They are called social insects. Termites, ants, and some bees and wasps are social insects. Some termites build huge mounds or nests. Most termites live in hot countries and feed on wood.

A new roof is added to these nests each year.

Jungle termite nests

Termite nest cut in half to show passages inside

Tree termite nest

Worker   Soldier

There are thousands of termites like these in each nest.

In tropical rain forests, where it rains a lot, termites build their nests with a roof. This works like an umbrella. It keeps heavy rain from damaging the nest.

In tropical South America, some termites build their nests in trees. This anteater uses its long, sticky tongue to reach in and eat the termites.

Queen

The queen lays eggs. The king fertilizes them.

King

Go to **www.usborne-quicklinks.com** for a link to a Web site where you can learn more about social insects and take an animated tour of a beehive.

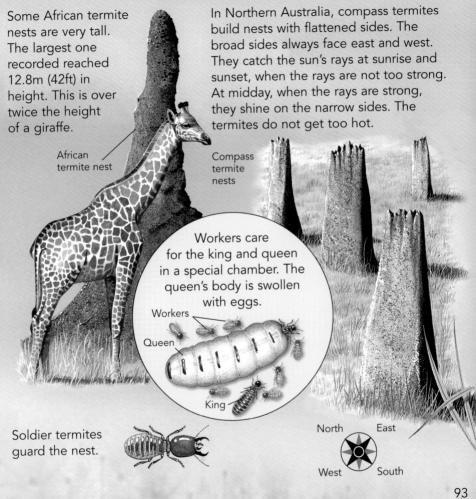

Some African termite nests are very tall. The largest one recorded reached 12.8m (42ft) in height. This is over twice the height of a giraffe.

African termite nest

In Northern Australia, compass termites build nests with flattened sides. The broad sides always face east and west. They catch the sun's rays at sunrise and sunset, when the rays are not too strong. At midday, when the rays are strong, they shine on the narrow sides. The termites do not get too hot.

Compass termite nests

Workers care for the king and queen in a special chamber. The queen's body is swollen with eggs.

Workers

Queen

King

Soldier termites guard the nest.

North East
West South

93

Amazing creepy crawlies

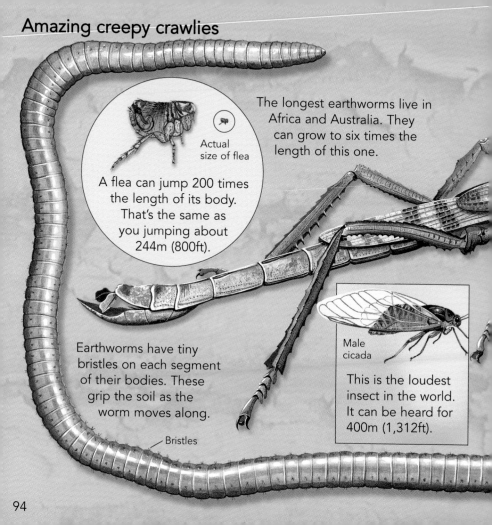

Actual size of flea

A flea can jump 200 times the length of its body. That's the same as you jumping about 244m (800ft).

The longest earthworms live in Africa and Australia. They can grow to six times the length of this one.

Earthworms have tiny bristles on each segment of their bodies. These grip the soil as the worm moves along.

Bristles

Male cicada

This is the loudest insect in the world. It can be heard for 400m (1,312ft).

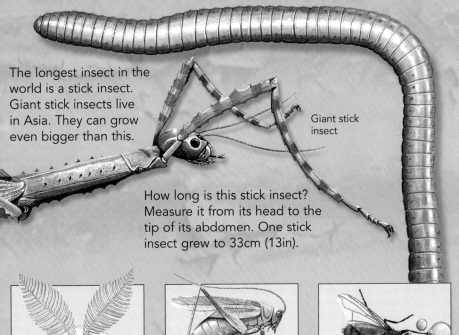

The longest insect in the world is a stick insect. Giant stick insects live in Asia. They can grow even bigger than this.

Giant stick insect

How long is this stick insect? Measure it from its head to the tip of its abdomen. One stick insect grew to 33cm (13in).

Luna moth

Moths can smell with their antennae.

Opening on leg

A cricket hears through openings near its "knees".

A fly tastes with its feet. It likes sweet, sugary foods best.

Go to www.usborne-quicklinks.com for a link to a Web site where you can find facts about many different creepy crawlies.

95

BUTTERFLIES
AND MOTHS

Rosamund Kidman Cox
Barbara Cork

Designed by David Bennett and Candice Whatmore
Cover design by Josephine Thompson
Cover illustration by Isabel Bowring

Illustrated by Joyce Bee, David Hurrell, Denise Finney,
Richard Lewington, Mick Loates,
Andy Martin, Dee Morgan, Liz Pepperell and Chris Shields

Edited by Laura Howell
Consultant editors: Anthony Wootton and David Carter
Language consultant: Betty Root

Contents

Looking at butterflies and moths

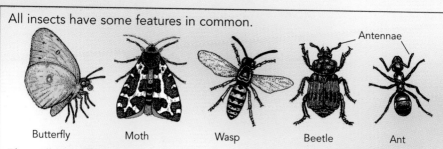

All insects have some features in common.

Butterfly   Moth   Wasp   Beetle   Antennae   Ant

They all have six legs and two antennae. Insects also have bodies which are divided into three parts – the head, thorax and abdomen.

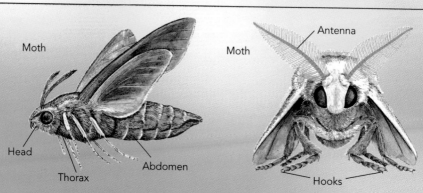

Moth

Head

Thorax

Abdomen

Moth

Antenna

Hooks

The thorax is the part of the body behind the head. The wings and legs join onto the thorax. The abdomen is the long part of the body.

Butterflies and moths have hooks on their feet for holding on tight. They feel and smell with their long antennae.

Go to **www.usborne-quicklinks.com** for a link to a Web site where you can find a friendly introduction to butterflies and moths.

Some insects have four wings, some have two wings and some have no wings. Butterflies and moths have four wings.

The wings are not joined together, but they move together when the butterfly flies.

Swallowtail butterfly

The front wings do most of the work. If they are damaged, the butterfly may not be able to fly properly.

If the back wings are damaged, the butterfly can still fly.

Looking at wings

Red underwing moth

When butterflies rest, they usually close their wings above their backs.

When moths rest, they fold their wings over their backs, or spread them out flat.

Oleander hawk moth

Common blue butterfly

The wings of a butterfly or moth are often bright on the top and duller underneath.

Privet hawk moth

When butterflies and moths rest, the dull shades on the outside of their wings make it hard for enemies to see them.

Walnut moth

Lappet moth

Scallop shell moth

Small skipper butterfly

Leaf butterfly

Buff-tip moth

Brimstone butterfly

Some butterflies look like leaves when they rest. They are hard to spot.

Some moths look like twigs when they rest. It is hard for enemies to see them.

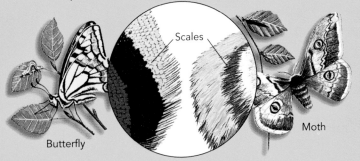
Scales

Butterfly

Moth

Red admiral butterfly

The patterns on a butterfly's or moth's wings are made of many tiny scales. If you touch the wings the scales will rub off.

Grayling butterfly

Green hairstreak butterfly

Monarch butterfly

Go to **www.usborne-quicklinks.com** for a link to a Web site where you can take a close-up look at a butterfly's body with many amazing microscope images.

101

Keeping warm and feeding

Butterflies and moths need to be warm for their bodies
to work properly. When the air is cold, they rest.

This butterfly, called a
Titania's fritillary, is
warming up
in the sun.

The dark parts
of the wings
warm up quickly.
Butterflies from
cold countries
often have dark
wings.

Moths are often very hairy.
The hairs on their bodies help
to keep them warm at night.

Flannel
moth

Moths often shiver before they
fly. The shivering helps to
warm up their bodies.

Elephant
hawk
moth

Go to www.usborne-quicklinks.com for a link to a Web site where you can find pictures and information
about keeping warm and feeding.

Butterflies and moths do not eat to grow larger. They use food to make heat inside their bodies. Heat makes energy. This keeps their bodies working.

Hummingbird hawk moth

Lime hawk moth

Moths may drink sap from trees or damaged plants.

Moths and butterflies drink a sweet liquid from flowers. This liquid is called nectar.

They drink nectar through a long tube called a proboscis.

Union jack butterfly

Proboscis

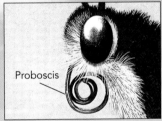

Proboscis

When butterflies and moths are not feeding, their proboscis is curled up.

Butterflies can taste with their feet.

103

A butterfly's day

Female common blue butterfly

1. The butterfly rests at night when it is cold.

2. When the sun comes out, she warms up.

3. She looks for a place to lay her eggs.

4. She lays her eggs on a particular plant.

5. She warms up again in the sun.

6. Now she is warm enough to fly away.

7. She lands on a flower to drink nectar.

8. When it gets dark and cold, she hides.

Go to www.usborne-quicklinks.com for a link to a Web site where you can find a selection of butterfly questions and answers.

A moth's night

1. The moth hides in the day when it is light.

2. At dusk he shivers to warm himself up.

3. Soon, he is ready to fly away and find a female.

4. He drinks some nectar from a flower.

5. Now it is very cold, so he rests.

6. When it gets warmer, he flies away again.

7. He finds a female and mates with her.

8. When it starts to get light, he hides.

Finding a partner

The most important thing that a butterfly or moth has to do is to find a partner for mating. When a female has mated she will lay her eggs.

Male

Scarce copper butterflies

Female

Male

Purple hairstreak butterflies

Female

Butterflies use patterns and shades to find each other.

Common blue butterflies

Female

Male

Sometimes the male looks different from the female. He may use his bright wings to show off to her.

Male

Male

Orange tip butterflies

Female

The male may have a home area. He will chase out other males and only allow females in.

Female

Male

Swallowtail butterflies

Female

Go to www.usborne-quicklinks.com for a link to a Web site where you can learn about butterflies' and moths' senses, which they use to find a partner.

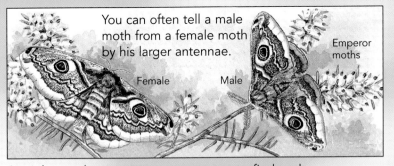

You can often tell a male moth from a female moth by his larger antennae.

Female   Male

Emperor moths

Male

Muslin moths

Female

At night, moths cannot use appearance to find each other. Instead the male finds the female by her scent. Each kind of moth has a different scent.

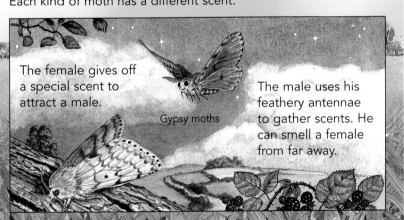

The female gives off a special scent to attract a male.

Gypsy moths

The male uses his feathery antennae to gather scents. He can smell a female from far away.

Male

Hag moths

Female   Oak eggar moths

Male

Female

Mating and laying eggs

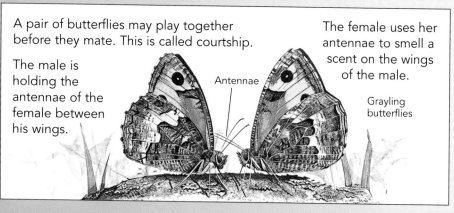

A pair of butterflies may play together before they mate. This is called courtship.

The male is holding the antennae of the female between his wings.

The female uses her antennae to smell a scent on the wings of the male.

Antennae

Grayling butterflies

When butterflies or moths mate, they join their abdomens together. A bag of sperm passes from the male to the female. The sperm joins with eggs inside the female. If they are frightened by an enemy, they sometimes fly away joined together.

Male

Female

Clouded yellow butterflies

Abdomen

Go to www.usborne-quicklinks for a link to a Web site where you can find the answers to many questions about butterflies and their eggs, with pictures, videos and animations.

A female may have hundreds of eggs inside her. She will lay her eggs when she has mated.

Bulrush wainscot moth

Abdomen

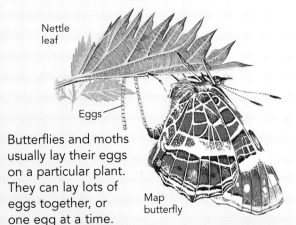

Nettle leaf

Eggs

Butterflies and moths usually lay their eggs on a particular plant. They can lay lots of eggs together, or one egg at a time.

Map butterfly

This moth lays each egg inside a bulrush. She makes holes in the stem with spines on the end of her abdomen.

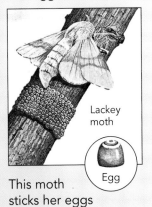

Lackey moth

Egg

This moth sticks her eggs to a twig.

Leopard moth

Egg

This moth sticks her eggs onto tree bark.

Marbled white butterfly

Egg

This butterfly lays her eggs as she flies.

The hungry caterpillar

A single caterpillar hatches out of each egg. It eats and eats, and grows and grows. When it is big enough to start changing into an adult butterfly or moth, it stops growing.

1. A moth caterpillar is inside this egg.

2. It eats a hole in the egg and crawls out.

3. It is very hungry, so it eats the old egg shell.

4. It eats the top of the leaf. Soon it grows too big for its own skin.

Old skin

5. The skin splits and the caterpillar wriggles out. It has grown a new skin.

Privet hawk moth caterpillar

6. This caterpillar eats privet leaves. It eats and grows and eats and grows. It changes skin three more times.

The caterpillar cannot see very well. It has twelve tiny eyes on its head. The eyes are too small for you to see.

Mouth parts for chewing

Front legs

Three pairs of front legs hold onto the food.

Five pairs of fleshy legs, called prolegs, can grip tightly to a stalk.

Air hole

Hooks

The caterpillar breathes through air holes in the side of its body. There is an air hole in the middle of each yellow spot.

Go to **www.usborne-quicklinks.com** for a link to a Web site where you can find lots of useful and easy-to-read information about caterpillars.

111

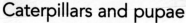

Caterpillars and pupae

This caterpillar makes a loop shape as it moves.

Marbled white butterfly caterpillar

When some caterpillars rest, they look like twigs. This helps them to hide from their enemies.

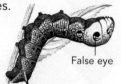

False eye

Some caterpillars are hairy. Birds do not like to eat them.

Some caterpillars have false eyes to frighten enemies.

Swallowtail butterfly caterpillar

Silk tent

Caterpillars

Caterpillars make silk from glands near their mouths. Some caterpillars use this silk to make tents to hide in.

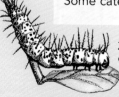

Zebra butterfly caterpillar

Lobster moth caterpillar

When caterpillars are fully grown, they change into pupae.

Peacock butterfly caterpillar

Old skin

Pupa

Cabbage white butterfly pupa

1. When this caterpillar is fully grown, it hangs upside down.

2. The caterpillar changes into a pupa inside its skin.

3. When the pupa wriggles, the skin splits and slides up the pupa.

Pupa

Silk cocoon

Some moth caterpillars bury themselves in the ground. Then they change into pupae.

Others spin silk cocoons. They change into pupae inside the cocoon.

Bagworm moth cocoon

4. The pupa skin is now hard. It has become paler, too.

Convolvulus hawk moth pupa

Orange tip butterfly pupa

Go to www.usborne-quicklinks.com for a link to a Web site where you can look at some photographs of pupae, and learn more about them.

The magic change

Inside a pupa, a butterfly or moth is made.

Monarch butterfly pupa

The abdomen is being made here.

One wing is being made here.

One antenna is being made here.

One eye is being made here.

1. This pupa is two days old. A monarch butterfly is being made inside it.

2. The pupa is now two weeks old. The butterfly is almost ready to come out.

The butterfly is pulling out its antennae, legs and proboscis.

3. The pupa skin splits. The head and legs of the butterfly come out first.

Go to **www.usborne-quicklinks.com** for a link to a Web site where you can look at photographs and descriptions of the stages in a butterfly's life.

The proboscis is in two parts.

At first the wings are crumpled.

Veins

4. The butterfly pulls out its abdomen. It pumps blood into the veins of its wings.

5. Blood is pumping from the abdomen into the veins. This makes the wings unfold.

6. The butterfly waits for its wings to dry and become stiff. Then it will be able to fly away.

The two parts of the proboscis join together to make a tube.

How long do they live?

A butterfly or moth goes through four stages in its life. Adult butterflies and moths usually live for only a few days or weeks. When they have mated and the female has laid her eggs, the adults die.

1. A butterfly or moth starts its life as an egg.

2. The egg changes into a caterpillar.

3. The caterpillar changes into a pupa.

4. The pupa changes into an adult.

In tropical countries, where the weather is always hot, a butterfly or moth often takes only a few weeks to change from an egg into an adult.

Go to **www.usborne-quicklinks.com** for a link to a Web site where you can search for photographs of butterflies that live in your country.

In colder countries, a butterfly or moth may take several months to change from an egg to an adult. In countries with very cold winters, they go into a deep sleep. They wake up when the weather gets warmer.

The lackey moth spends the winter as an egg.

The herald moth sleeps through the winter as an adult.

The cabbage white butterfly spends the winter as a pupa.

The privet hawk moth spends the winter as a pupa in the soil.

The marbled white butterfly sleeps through the winter as a young caterpillar.

Butterflies and moths that spend part of their lives sleeping through the winter may take up to a year to change from an egg to an adult.

Enemies

Butterflies and moths have lots of enemies.

Birds eat them.

Spiders eat them.

Insects eat them.

At night, many moths are eaten by bats.

Some moths have ears on the sides of their bodies. These help them to hear the squeaks that bats make. If these moths hear a bat coming, they drop to the ground or try to dodge out of the way.

Blue underwing moth

Some butterflies and moths use tricks or warnings to frighten away enemies.

Red underwing moth

If an enemy disturbs this moth, it opens and closes its wings. The flash of red may frighten away the enemy.

Owl butterfly

This butterfly has markings like eyes on its wings. Birds may think they are the eyes of a dangerous animal.

Cinnabar moth

Cinnabar moth caterpillar

Tiger moth

Most butterflies and moths that are red and black, or yellow and black, taste bad. Birds learn not to eat them.

At night, tiger moths make clicking noises. Bats soon learn that moths that make this noise taste bad.

Go to www.usborne-quicklinks.com for a link to a Web site where you can learn about the many different tricks butterflies use to defend themselves.

119

FLOWERS

Rosamund Kidman Cox
Barbara Cork

Designed by David Bennett
and Candice Whatmore
Cover design by Josephine Thompson
Cover illustration by Isabel Bowring

Illustrated by Wendy Bramall, Mark Burgess,
Michelle Emblem, Denise Finney, Sarah Fox-Davies,
Sheila Galbraith, Victoria Gooman, David Hurrell, Mick Loates,
Andy Martin, Dee Morgan, Cynthia Pow and Ralph Stobart

Edited by Laura Howell
Consultant editor: Mary Gibby Ph.D.
Language consultant: Betty Root

Contents

Looking at flowers

If you look closely at a flower, you will see that it is made of many different parts.

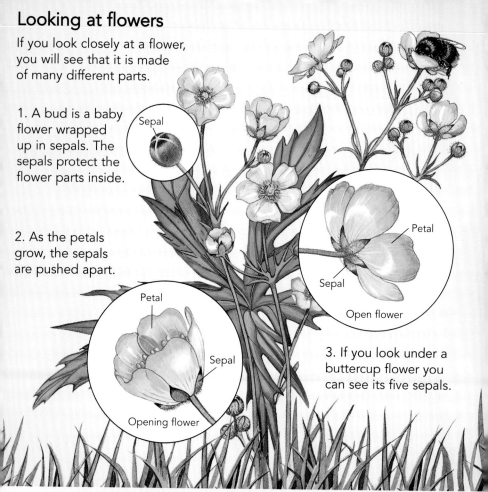

1. A bud is a baby flower wrapped up in sepals. The sepals protect the flower parts inside.

Sepal

2. As the petals grow, the sepals are pushed apart.

Petal

Sepal

Opening flower

Petal

Sepal

Open flower

3. If you look under a buttercup flower you can see its five sepals.

Go to **www.usborne-quicklinks.com** for a link to a Web site where you can learn about plant life by solving the mystery of the Great Plant Escape.

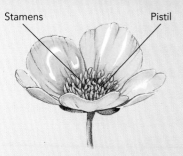

Stamens
Pistil

Inside the ring of petals are more flower parts. The green parts in the middle are called the pistil. Around it are the stamens.

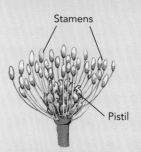

Stamens
Pistil

If you remove the petals and sepals, you can see all the parts inside.

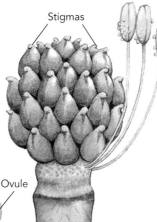

Each part of the pistil has a sticky top called a stigma.

Stigmas

Stamen

Pollen

There is a tiny ovule inside each part of the pistil. It will grow into a seed.

Ovule

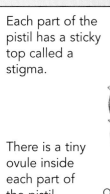

The top of each stamen holds yellow dust called pollen.

Looking at flower parts

Most types of flowers have the same parts, but they may seem very different. You need to look closely at each flower to see which part is which.

Bindweed

Harebell

Some have petals of different shapes and sizes.

Violet

Some flowers have petals joined together.

Lily

Bottlebrush

Some have lots of stamens.

Some have bright sepals and petals.

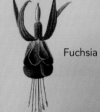

Fuchsia

Pink

Vetch

Columbine

Go to www.usborne-quicklinks.com for a link to a Web site where you can examine many flowers, and spot how their petals and sepals are different.

Stigma

Some flowers have a pistil with only one stigma.

Daffodil

Stigmas

Some have a pistil with more than one stigma.

Crocus

Cranesbill

An aster flower is made of lots of tiny flowers.

In the middle of the aster are many tiny yellow flowers.

Each flower around the outside has one long petal.

Daisy

There is a bumblebee somewhere on this page. Do you know why it visits flowers? The answer is on the next page.

Dandelion

Dahlia

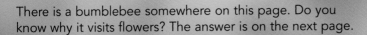

125

Flower visitors

Cranesbill

Flowers have many visitors. They are usually insects, such as bees. Bumblebees visit flowers to drink a sweet liquid called nectar. Sometimes the visitors eat some of the flower's pollen.

Yellow flag

A visitor to this flower needs a long tongue to reach down to the nectar.

Many flowers have guide lines or dots that point the way to the nectar.

Nectar is in here.

126

Pink

Most flowers are very bright and have a powerful scent so visitors can find them. Butterflies like to visit pink, red and blue flowers.

Honeysuckle

Most moths drink nectar at night. They visit flowers that have a sweet scent. These flowers are easy to find in the dark.

The flowers help the visitors by giving them food. The visitors also help the flowers. Do you know what the visitors do? The answer is on the next page.

This Australian honey possum is drinking nectar.

Gum tree flower

Stamen

Nectar is at the bottom of the stamens.

Go to **www.usborne-quicklinks.com** for a link to a Web site where you can find a detailed description of the tricks flowers use to attract visitors. Lots of pictures.

127

Why do flowers need visitors?

Visitors help plants by moving pollen from flower to flower.

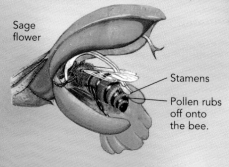

Sage flower

Stamens

Pollen rubs off onto the bee.

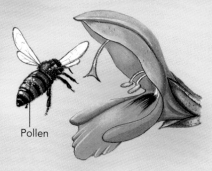

Pollen

1. As a bee collects nectar from a flower, its body gets covered with pollen.

2. It flies to another sage flower. It has pollen from the first flower on its back.

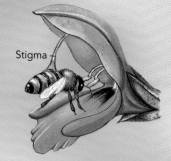

Stigma

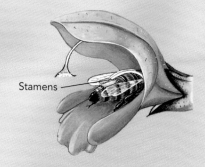

Stamens

3. As it lands, the pollen on the bee's body rubs onto the stigma of the flower.

4. The bee goes into the flower. New pollen from the stamens rubs onto its back.

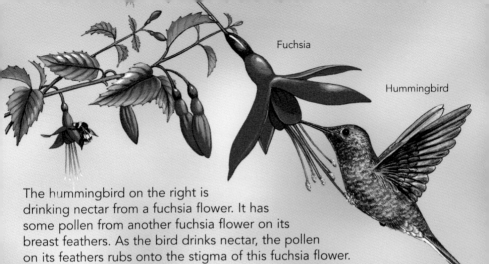

Fuchsia

Hummingbird

The hummingbird on the right is drinking nectar from a fuchsia flower. It has some pollen from another fuchsia flower on its breast feathers. As the bird drinks nectar, the pollen on its feathers rubs onto the stigma of this fuchsia flower.

Watching for visitors

Find a flower that has stamens and a stigma that are easy to see. When the sun is out, sit down and wait quietly for the insects to come.

Tulip

When the insect flies away, look to see if it has left any pollen on the stigma of your flower.

If an insect comes, try to see if it has any pollen on its body.

Go to www.usborne-quicklinks.com for a link to a Web site where you can find out which flowers attract different kinds of butterflies.

Plantain flowers

False oat grass flowers

How the wind helps flowers

The flowers on this page do not need visitors to move their pollen. The wind blows it from flower to flower.

These flowers have no scent or bright petals to attract visitors.

Plantain

Instead, they have many stamens with lots of pollen. The wind blows it away.

In the spring, you may see clouds of pollen blowing off grass flowers. Most of this pollen will be wasted, but some will stick onto the stigmas of other grass flowers.

Wood-rush flowers

Rye flowers

Go to www.usborne-quicklinks.com for a link to a Web site where you can find out lots about seeds, nuts and fruits, and how they are scattered.

All trees have flowers. Many trees use the wind to move their pollen.

The walnut tree has two kinds of flowers. One kind of flower has a large pistil.

The other kind of flower is made of lots of stamens.

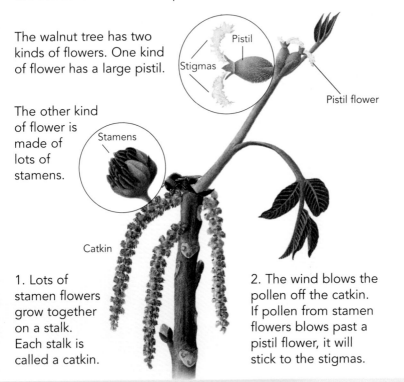

Pistil

Stigmas

Pistil flower

Stamens

Catkin

1. Lots of stamen flowers grow together on a stalk. Each stalk is called a catkin.

2. The wind blows the pollen off the catkin. If pollen from stamen flowers blows past a pistil flower, it will stick to the stigmas.

Pistil flower

Hazel tree flowers

Stamen flowers

Larch tree flowers

Stamen flowers

Pistil flowers

131

What happens to the pollen?

1. A bee has left pollen on this flower's stigma. The pollen came from another poppy flower.

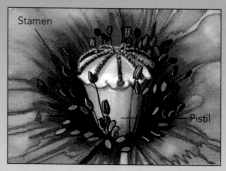

2. Each grain of pollen grows a tube down inside the pistil. There are tiny, egg-like ovules inside the pistil.

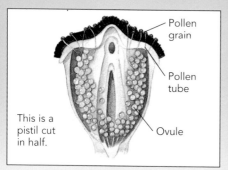

This is a pistil cut in half.

3. When a tube reaches an ovule, the inside of the pollen grain moves down the tube and joins with the ovule.

Seeds grow in here.

The petals and stamens die.

4. The ovules in the pistil have been fertilized by the pollen. The fertilized ovules will grow into poppy seeds.

Go to www.usborne-quicklinks.com for a link to a Web site where you can watch a short animated movie about pollination.

The flowers on the poppy plant can be fertilized only when an insect brings pollen from another poppy plant.

A poppy flower cannot use its own pollen to fertilize its own ovules. The pollen will not grow tubes down into the pistil.

Poppy pollen will not grow tubes in a buttercup pistil.

Buttercup flowers

More about pollen

Most flowers are like the poppy. They do not use their own pollen to fertilize themselves. Pollen must be brought from another flower of the same kind by visitors or by the wind.

A single flower of the yellow mountain saxifrage below can never fertilize itself because the stamens die before the stigmas are ripe.

Stamens

No stigmas

Stigmas

Old stamen

The flowers on this plant are less than a week old. Only the stamens are ripe.

The flowers on this plant are more than eleven days old. The stigmas are ripe, but the stamens are dead.

Go to www.usborne-quicklinks.com for a link to a Web site where you can find pictures, information and video clips of pollen being carried from flowers.

The pollen of this bee orchid is moved only by male Eucera bees. But if no Eucera bees visit the orchid it will use its own pollen to fertilize itself.

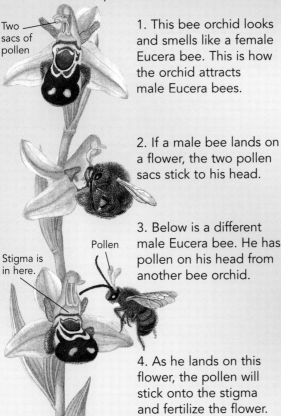

Two sacs of pollen

Stigma is in here.

Pollen

1. This bee orchid looks and smells like a female Eucera bee. This is how the orchid attracts male Eucera bees.

2. If a male bee lands on a flower, the two pollen sacs stick to his head.

3. Below is a different male Eucera bee. He has pollen on his head from another bee orchid.

4. As he lands on this flower, the pollen will stick onto the stigma and fertilize the flower.

If no bees visit this bee orchid, it will fertilize itself.

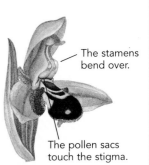

The stamens bend over.

The pollen sacs touch the stigma.

This is how the bee orchid fertilizes itself.

How seeds leave the plant

1. The ovules in this poppy pistil have been fertilized. They are growing into seeds.

2. The pistil swells. It is now a fruit with seeds inside.

3. Holes open in the top. When the wind blows the fruit, the seeds fall out.

The fruit has now dried up and died.

Looking inside a seed

If you split open a bean seed, this is what you will see inside.

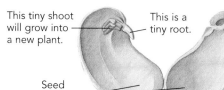

This tiny shoot will grow into a new plant.

This is a tiny root.

Seed leaves

This is a bean seed. It has a thick skin to protect the parts inside.

These are two seed leaves, which are full of food. The shoot will use this food when it grows.

Go to www.usborne-quicklinks.com for a link to a Web site where you can look at different kinds of fruits and seeds, with helpful diagrams.

When the seeds in the fruits are ripe, the wind or animals may move them away from the plant.

Birds eat fruits and drop the seeds.

Maple tree fruits spin to the ground because of their special shape.

Sometimes animals bury fruits to eat later. The seeds that do not get eaten may grow into new plants.

The cranesbill fruit springs open and its seeds fly out.

The wind blows away the dandelion fruits.

Buttercup fruits may catch onto the fur of animals.

Plants make lots of seeds but only a few of them will grow into new plants. The others die or get eaten.

137

How a seed grows

1. Autumn
A bird drops a sunflower seed by accident.

2. Winter
The seed falls to the ground and gets covered over.

3. Spring
Rain makes the seed swell. A root grows down into the soil.

4. Spring
The shoot grows up to the light.

Seed leaves

5. Spring

Proper leaves start to grow. They will make food.

The baby plant uses the food in the seed leaves to grow.

The root takes water and minerals from the soil.

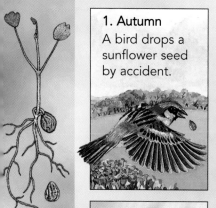

Nasturtium

Pea

Oak acorn

Sycamore

Go to **www.usborne-quicklinks.com** for a link to a Web site where you can learn more about sunflowers and how they grow.

6. Late spring

The sunflower plant grows a flower bud. The plant is now taller than a person.

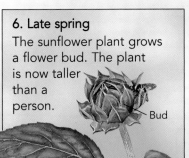

Bud

7. Summer

The bud opens. Bees bring pollen from other sunflowers.

8. Autumn

The flowers have been fertilized.

A bird eats the seeds.

The seeds pass through the bird's body, fall to the ground, and the process begins again.

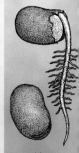

Broad bean

Maize

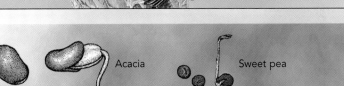

Acacia

Sweet pea

How insects help flowers

Flowers make most nectar and scent when their pistil or stamens are ripe, because this is when they need to attract visitors.

Bees visit these cherry flowers in the morning. This is when the flowers have most nectar.

New honeysuckle flowers open in the evening. This is when moths visit them.

Bees visit these apple flowers in the afternoon. This is when the flowers have most nectar.

The flowers make lots of scent in the evening, but only a little scent in the day.

Go to www.usborne-quicklinks.com for a link to a Web site where you can find detailed information about how and why plants attract insects.

Many plants take several weeks to open all their flowers. Bees come back to these plants day after day until all the flowers have opened.

The willowherb takes about a month to open all its flowers. The first flowers to open are at the bottom of the stem. The last flowers to open are at the top of the stem.

Willowherb (also known as fireweed)

New horse chestnut tree flowers open every day. They have lots of nectar. Yellow guide lines point the way to the nectar.

New guide lines

Old guide lines

When the nectar is finished the guide lines turn red. Bees do not visit old flowers with red guide lines.

As each flower gets older, it makes more nectar. Bees always visit older willowherb flowers first.

141

Keeping pollen safe

Most flowers try to keep their pollen safe and dry. Cold weather, rain and dew could damage the pollen or wash it away.

When flowers are closed, the pollen is kept safe.

Pasque flower

Crocus

When flowers are closed, rain and dew cannot get inside.

Ox-eye daisy

Daisy

These flowers come out in early spring. The flowers open only when it is warm and sunny. If the sun goes in, they close up their petals. The flowers open again when the sun comes out.

These flowers close in the evening and in bad weather. If they have to stay closed for several days, they will fertilize themselves.

Go to www.usborne-quicklinks.com for a link to a Web site where you can find amazing facts about plants and flowers.

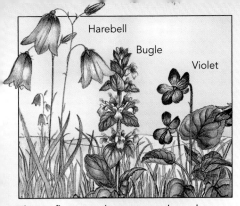

These flowers do not need to close their petals to keep the pollen safe. Water cannot collect inside them.

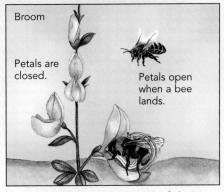

The stamens and the pistil of the broom flower are kept safe inside the petals. They spring out when a bee lands on the bottom petals.

Ripe stamens of apple tree flowers split open to let out the pollen. The stamens will split open only on warm days.

New catchfly flowers open in the evening. This is when moths visit them. If the evenings are very cold, no new flowers will open.

143

TREES

Ruth Thomson

Designed by David Bennett
and Nicky Wainwright
Cover design by Josephine Thompson

Illustrated by Bob Bampton,
Wendy Bramall, Paul Brooks,
Frankie Coventry, Sarah Fox-Davies,
Mick Loates, Andy Martin, Dee McLean,
David More, Ralph Stobart, Sally Voke
and James Woods

Edited by Laura Howell
Consultant editor: Esmond Harris B.Sc., Dip.For., F.I.For.
Language consultant: Betty Root

Contents

Amazing facts about trees

Trees are the largest plants in the world. They also live the longest.

On a warm day in spring, a large tree like this takes up enough water from the soil to fill five bathtubs.

Trees cover about one third of the Earth's land surface.

Sometimes, the roots of a tree spread wider than its branches.

146

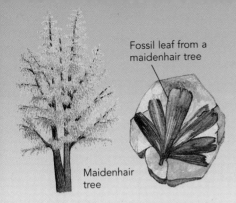

Fossil leaf from a maidenhair tree

Maidenhair tree

Maidenhair trees today look almost the same as the ones that grew 200 million years ago.

Bristlecone pine tree

This type of tree lives for a long time. The oldest one is over 4,750 years old.

This sierra redwood tree grows in California, North America.

People say that this tree has enough wood to make all these buildings. It is the biggest tree in the world. It is 83m (272ft) tall and 24m (79ft) around the trunk.

Go to **www.usborne-quicklinks.com** for a link to a Web site where you can discover what makes trees and forests so fascinating, and play a match-a-leaf game.

147

Trees in the countryside

This picture shows some of the places where trees grow. Some of them grow naturally and others are planted by people.

This is a windy hillside. The branches of the trees grow bent over because of the wind.

Trees in woods grow close together. They have thin trunks and not very many lower branches.

People sometimes plant trees around their houses to protect them from wind and frost.

A tree growing on its own has spreading branches.

Some trees grow near water.

Go to www.usborne-quicklinks.com for a link to a Web site where you can explore a fantastic forest in an interactive adventure.

Few trees can grow on the hilltops. It is too cold and windy.

Foresters plant pine and spruce trees in straight lines. These trees grow very quickly.

Trees are sometimes planted near roads to give shade.

Every few years, some trees in the forest are cut down. This gives the stronger trees more room to grow.

Trees often mark the edges of fields. They also stop the soil from blowing away.

Under the ground

Roots help a tree in many ways. They take up water and minerals from the soil. A tree needs these things to grow. Roots hold the tree in place and they also hold the soil together. On steep ground, they help stop the soil from washing away in the rain.

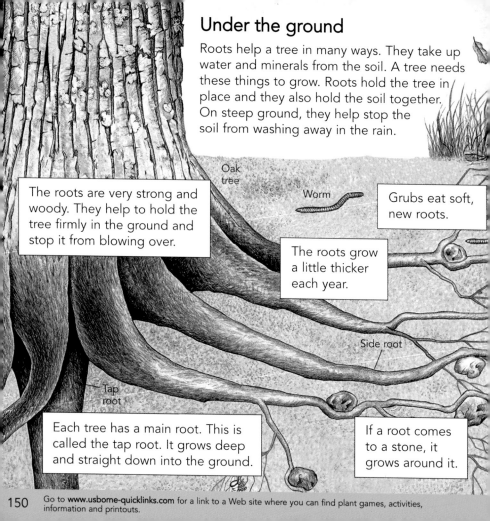

Oak tree

Worm

Grubs eat soft, new roots.

The roots are very strong and woody. They help to hold the tree firmly in the ground and stop it from blowing over.

The roots grow a little thicker each year.

Side root

Tap root

Each tree has a main root. This is called the tap root. It grows deep and straight down into the ground.

If a root comes to a stone, it grows around it.

Go to **www.usborne-quicklinks.com** for a link to a Web site where you can find plant games, activities, information and printouts.

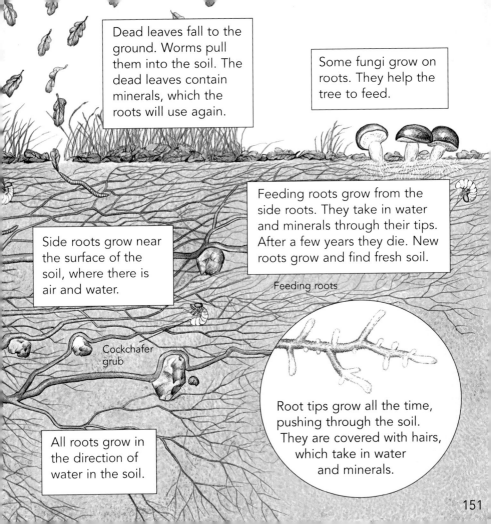

Dead leaves fall to the ground. Worms pull them into the soil. The dead leaves contain minerals, which the roots will use again.

Some fungi grow on roots. They help the tree to feed.

Feeding roots grow from the side roots. They take in water and minerals through their tips. After a few years they die. New roots grow and find fresh soil.

Feeding roots

Side roots grow near the surface of the soil, where there is air and water.

Cockchafer grub

Root tips grow all the time, pushing through the soil. They are covered with hairs, which take in water and minerals.

All roots grow in the direction of water in the soil.

151

How a twig grows

This is how a beech twig grows in one year.

1. Winter

In winter, the bare twigs on the tree begin to grow buds. These will become new stems and leaves.

Leading bud

Side buds

This is the leading bud. It is covered with scales that protect it. The new stem and leaves are inside the scales.

Side shoots

The side buds grow into side shoots.

2. Spring

The new stem grows and the leaves unfold. The scales are pushed apart. The new leaves are soft and pale.

New leaf

Go to **www.usborne-quicklinks.com** for a link to a Web site where you can take a look at a year in the life of a tree, including how its parts grow.

3. Summer

By summer, the stems are stiff and the leaves are dark green and shiny.

New leading bud

New bud

At the end of summer, a new bud is made just above each leaf stalk. Next year, this bud will grow into a new side shoot.

4. Autumn

When the twig stops growing, it makes a new leading bud. Next spring, this bud will grow into a new shoot.

The leaves turn brown before they fall off.

Girdle scar, where leading bud was in winter

The leading bud scales leave a mark called a girdle scar. If you count the girdle scars on a twig, you can find out how old the twig is. This twig is two years old.

Tree stumps

This is the inside of a healthy tree stump. Most of it is sapwood. This carries water and minerals up from the roots to the leaves.

In the middle is heartwood. It is made of old, dead sapwood. It is very hard and strong.

Bark stops the tree from drying out and protects it from insects and disease. Bark cannot stretch. It splits or peels as the wood inside grows. New bark grows underneath.

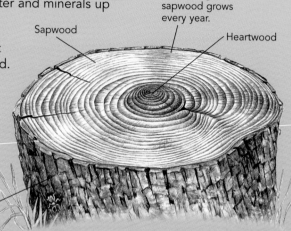

A new ring of sapwood grows every year.

Sapwood

Heartwood

Bark

Although trees are strong, they may die if fungus attacks them.

Spores

1. Fungus spores in the air get into a wound in the tree.

2. The fungus spreads inside the trunk. The heartwood rots.

The heartwood in this tree is rotten.

3. When the tree gets weak inside, it falls over in a storm.

Go to **www.usborne-quicklinks.com** for a link to a Web site where you can learn more about the different parts of a tree stump.

When a tree dies, the bark becomes loose. Animals and plants can get under the bark. Many of them feed on the rotting wood.

Bracket fungi grow on the trunk and feed on the rotting wood.

Slugs eat dead leaves and fungi. In dry weather they hide in cracks under the bark.

Longhorn beetle

Scarlet cup fungi

Bark beetles and their grubs make long tunnels under the bark.

Centipedes live under the bark. They come out at night to hunt for small insects.

Woodlice hide in damp places under the bark. They feed on rotting wood.

Millipedes live on the ground. They feed on dead leaves.

Deciduous tree leaves

Many trees are deciduous. This means that they lose their leaves in autumn. Most deciduous trees have soft, flat leaves.

These are lime leaves. Lime trees lose their leaves in autumn.

Lime tree

Rowan

Vein

Veins make the leaf stiff. Water and food travel through them.

The top side faces the sun.

Holes on underside of leaf

Leaf stalk

Oak

The leaf stalk can bend so that the leaf does not break on windy days. Water and food travel through it.

There are hundreds of tiny holes on the leaf's underside. These open and close to let air in and out and water out.

Sycamore

Quaking aspen

Horse chestnut

Go to **www.usborne-quicklinks.com** for a link to a Web site where you can find out about a type of evergreen tree called a conifer, with facts and things to do.

Evergreen tree leaves

Trees that keep their leaves all winter are called evergreens. Most evergreens have tough, waxy leaves.

Pine trees have evergreen leaves. Pine leaves are long and narrow. They can stay alive in winter because they are tough and thick. Their waxy skin stops them from drying out. They can still make some food in winter.

Pine leaf

Evergreen leaf veins are in lines.

Italian cypress

Snow gum

Monterey pine

An evergreen tree keeps its leaves for several years. Then they turn brown and fall off. Unlike deciduous trees, they do not fall off all at once. The tree always has some leaves.

Leaves have many different shapes, but they all do the same work. You can find out what they do on the next page.

Norway spruce

Juniper

Evergreen oak

Scots pine

157

What leaves do

A tree breathes and feeds with its leaves. Start at the bottom of the page and follow the numbers to see how a tree makes its food.

4. A green chemical in leaves makes food from air and water during the daytime.

3. The leaves take in air.

2. The water travels up the trunk through tubes in the sapwood.

5. The food moves around the tree in special tubes. These tubes are just under the bark.

Water

Food

1. The roots take up water from the soil.

Go to **www.usborne-quicklinks.com** for a link to a Web site where you can watch a short animated movie about autumn leaves.

Why do deciduous trees lose their leaves in autumn?

Silver maple

1. In autumn, it is not warm enough for leaves to make much food. Cold weather would damage soft leaves.

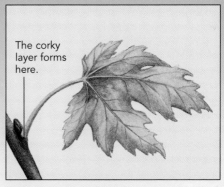

The corky layer forms here.

2. A corky layer grows across the leaf stalk. Water cannot get to the leaf any more. The leaf changes shade.

This is a new leaf bud. Below it is the scar where the leaf was joined to the twig.

3. The leaf dries out and dies. The wind blows it off the tree.

4. All the leaves fall off. The tree rests until spring.

Tree flowers

All trees have flowers, even if you don't notice them. Flowers have stamens which hold pollen, and a pistil which holds ovules. Pollen that lands on the top of the pistil grows down to join with the ovules. This is called fertilization. Fertilized ovules grow into seeds.

1. The petals and scent of these flowers attract insects. They feed on a sweet liquid called nectar inside the flower.

This is a stamen. It makes a dust called pollen.

Honey bee

The top of the pistil is called the stigma. Pollen sticks to it.

2. When an insect comes to feed, it brushes against the stamens. Pollen rubs onto its body.

3. When it visits a flower on another tree, the pollen is brushed onto the stigma. The flower can now make seeds.

Go to **www.usborne-quicklinks.com** for a link to a Web site where you can find a friendly and detailed explanation of what flowers do.

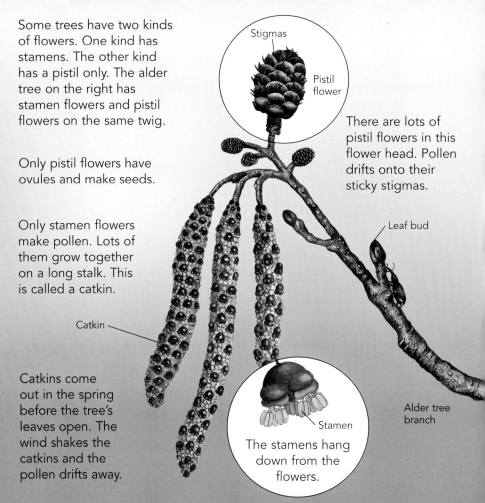

Some trees have two kinds of flowers. One kind has stamens. The other kind has a pistil only. The alder tree on the right has stamen flowers and pistil flowers on the same twig.

Only pistil flowers have ovules and make seeds.

Only stamen flowers make pollen. Lots of them grow together on a long stalk. This is called a catkin.

Catkins come out in the spring before the tree's leaves open. The wind shakes the catkins and the pollen drifts away.

Stigmas

Pistil flower

There are lots of pistil flowers in this flower head. Pollen drifts onto their sticky stigmas.

Leaf bud

Catkin

Alder tree branch

Stamen

The stamens hang down from the flowers.

161

Fruits and seeds

The fertilized ovules grow into seeds. Fruits grow to hold and protect them.

Cherry

Seed

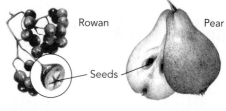
Rowan

Seeds

Pear

These fruits are soft and juicy. Birds and animals eat them. Some have only one seed inside, others have lots.

Horse chestnut

Seed

Willow

Seed

Hornbeam

Seed is in here.

Wing

This fruit is spiky. It protects the seed inside.

This fruit is made up of lots of seeds with feathery tops.

This fruit is hard and dry. It has a leafy wing.

Birch

Beech

Hazel

Sitka spruce

Lime

Plane

Go to **www.usborne-quicklinks.com** for a link to a Web site where you can find lots of facts about many different kinds of fruits.

Many evergreen trees have fruits called cones. The flowers that grow at the tips of new shoots grow into cones. Sometimes this takes two years.

Pine flowers are made up of soft scales. Each scale has two ovules inside. When pollen lands on the ovules they start to change into seeds. The scales close up to protect the seeds.

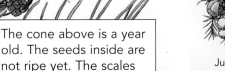

Ovules

A pine flower cut in half

Pine flower

Yew

The cone above is a year old. The seeds inside are not ripe yet. The scales are hard and tightly shut.

Juniper

The cone on the left is two years old. It is large and woody. The seeds inside are ripe. On a dry day, the scales open and the seeds fall out.

Crab apple

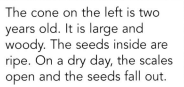

Scots pine

Seeds

Mulberry

Sweet chestnut

Black locust

163

How seeds are moved

When the seeds in fruits are ripe, the wind or animals may move them away from the tree. This is because there is not enough light under the parent tree for seedlings to grow well.

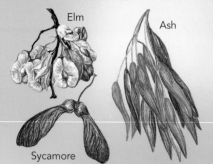

Elm

Ash

Sycamore

Fruits with "wings" spin away from the tree.

Falling acorn

Jay

Oak tree

Plane

White poplar

Some fruits are very light. They have tiny hairs that help them float away in the wind.

Squirrels carry acorns away from oak trees and bury them. Birds feed on acorns and drop some. A few of these acorns will grow into trees.

Go to **www.usborne-quicklinks.com** for a link to a Web site where you can find out how the seeds of some types of trees are moved.

Birds carry the fruits and seeds away from these trees. They eat the fruits and drop the seeds.

Fieldfare

Holly

Blackthorn

Dogwood

Elder

Hawthorn

Waxwing

Alder cone

Seeds

Alder trees grow near water. Their seeds drop in the water and float away. Some seeds will be washed up on a damp river bank. They may grow into new trees.

Look for willow fruits in spring and summer.

Willow fruits

Poplar hawk moth

This moth is a similar shade to the trunk. It is hard to spot.

Leaf beetle

Look for beetles on the leaves and flowers.

Birds often visit trees to nest or sleep. Some search for seeds or insects.

Red underwing moth

Some moths live on willow trees. They rest in the day and fly away at night.

Index

First published in 2003 by Usborne Publishing Ltd., Usborne House, 83-85 Saffron Hill, London EC1N 8RT, England.
www.usborne.com Copyright © 2003, 1990, 1980 Usborne Publishing Ltd.